Who *is* This GOD?

The Story of
the Creator, Angels, and People
in Theology, Mythology, and History

Marcus O. Durham, PhD
Rosemary Durham

Dream Point Publishers
Tulsa

Who Is This God?

Contact:
THEWAY Corp.
P.O. Box 33124
Tulsa, OK 74153

www.ThewayCorp.com

Editor: Sarah Durham Coffin, Cairns of Stone, Jenks, OK.
Cover Design: Jason Maddox, ThinkDesignCo, Tulsa, OK.
Research: Karen Durham Wisdom, The Vine, Oklahoma City, OK.

Printed in United States of America
First printing by Fidlar Doubleday, May 2002
Second printing by Fidlar Doubleday, February 2003
Second edition, February 2012

Library of Congress Control Number: 2002091075

ISBN 0-9719324-0-9

Copyright © 2002-2012 by Marcus O. Durham

Others Say: The book is for everyone.

In over 50 years of ministry, I have encountered many good books on theology. *Who Is This God?* surpasses those and is an excellent work for seekers, agnostics, and those who are not quite sure what they believe. It is excellent for those who want to know about the study in a practical, real way.
  - Dr. Clifford E. Clark, International Missions Leader and Popular Conference Speaker

I have just completed your excellent and informative book, *Who Is This God?* Our Sunday School class was beginning a course on this very subject and I held off starting your book until the class started the course. I felt that if I read your book as we went through the class I could at least appear to be more informed on the subject than I normally would have—and I was. It was obvious that you put a great deal of research into your ideas and the fruit of that research was apparent in the final product. I hope your book is doing well because it is well written and well documented.
  - David W. Davis, Attorney at Law

Thank you for your insightful, thought provoking study *Who is This God?* The book answers many questions about God and His creation and stimulates its reader to spiritual self-examination. I consider *Who is This God?* a valuable resource of biblical truth.
  - Mary Bales, Secretary

What a great book. Too often, the Body of Christ over-spiritualizes and complicates things. It is so refreshing to see a book that takes the message and breaks it down in a relevant fashion. I have found in my communication that the more practical my message is the greater the response. Jesus is so practical. He used illustrations and spoke in a very real way. This book goes right in that same direction.
  - Rev. Eastman Curtis, Senior Pastor, Destiny Church

Thanks for the gracious comments.
  - The Authors

Table of Contents

1. **What Is Your Background?**...11
   What are you talking about – Culture – Outside effect –
   Language – Translation – Who is on first – Guiding principles

2. **Icon, Image, and Likeness**..19
   Back to basics – Man is an icon – Like who – Science accord –
   God is in the details – Pattern of analysis

3. **Can You Count to Three?**..25
   Pattern – Check the original language – Retranslate – Location,
   location, location – Mind over matter – Word pictures – What
   about theology – Contemplation – A little history

4. **Name That God**..35
   Pattern – A majority of one, God – Hovering, Spirit – What is
   proper, Yehovah – What is that sir, Lord – What is in a name –
   Associations

5. **Nicknames, Combos, and Specials**.......................................41
   Names mean things – El combo – Yehovah combo – I Am –
   With us – The concepts

6. **Attributes Are the Ultimate**...47
   Structure – Philosophy category – Perfect – Unique – Infinite –
   Fun with numbers – Science category – Stable – Perpetual –
   Everywhere – Personality category – Absolute – Self-sufficient
   – All-knowing – What does it all mean

7. **What a Character**..59
   Society needs – Where from – Personal application – Virtue –
   Morality – Integrity

8. **More Character**...65
   Expanding an idea – Internal: Compassion – Charisma – Calm –
   Horizontal: Patience – Kindness – Virtue – Vertical:
   Confidence – Gentleman – Control – Legal: Legal concepts
   Mercy – Just – Free – Relating an application

v

9. **In the Name of Jesus**... 77
History pivot – What is the proper name, Jesus – Annointed,
Christ – A hovering, Spirit – A title, Lord – A full house – I Am
– Your commission – A composite picture – The final curtain

10. **Titles, Tags, and Terms**... 91
What's up – Forecast – Other names

11. **Genealogy 101 – Pre-Deluge**................................. 107
History pivot – Messianic prophecy and promise – History
repeats itself – What about ages – Ussher in time – The spitting
image – For whom the bell tolls – A notable exception –
Ancient of ancients – Preparation for a new beginning – Favor
in the eyes – Father of us all – Why the tree

12. **Genealogy 201 – Linguistics**................................... 123
History repeats – Human government – Archaeology and
history – The boys – Shem, Ham, and Japheth – Where did the
big group go – Where did the other travelers go – Dynasties –
The home boys – All for one and one for all – Pangaea – Time
and again – Coming of age – Mythology and Melchizadek –
One family only

13. **Genealogy 301 – Royalty**.. 141
A new celebrity – Leaving Chaldea – A new dispensation –
Isaac – Jacob – Judah – From Egypt – Kinsman redeemer – The
King has entered the building – The wisest man – The royals –
The family line – The merger – Royal line to Joseph – Bloodline
to Mary – Deity line of father – Dispensation

14. **Spirit Is in the Air**... 155
Third study – Always there – Guiding – Protector – Positive
attitude – Control model – Change of control – Change point –
Good old days – Ask and receive

15. **Angels – Spirits of Another Kind**........................... 165
Variety of life – Realms – Angel created – Order in the court –
Relations branch – Service branch – Personal branch – Named
ones – Deuterocanonical – Timing – Procreation – Left home – I
will – Center of the earth – Light versus darkness – Super
majority

16. **Other Gods** 183
   The tale tells – Early time – What manner of person is this –
   Nimrod – Egypt – Online encyclopedia – The Greek titans –
   The Greek Olympians – Israel foreigners – What is next

17. **Angel of the Lord** 193
   Another angel – Could it be – Contact – Guardians – Spirit
   condition

18. **Gifts of Spirit** 199
   Talents – Operation – Search – Miracle workers – Be well –
   Service – Language – Free indeed

19. **Spirit Influence** 209
   Check the spirits – Positive attitude – Positive or negative fruit –
   Weigh every thought – It's your money – Come again

20. **Who Is This God to You?** 217
   It's your choice – Planetary changes – Life cycle of faults –
   Meddling – Ignorance – The rest of the story – Stimulus –
   Charisma – More stimuli – Why do bad things happen to good
   people – Vulnerable

21. **Recap** 231
   Foundations – Triad – Attributes – Character – In the name of
   Jesus – Spirit – Spirit of another kind – Other gods – Angel of
   the Lord and other spirits – Review – Capstone

   References 227

   Authors 229

⇐ ⇑ ⇒

Preface

Everything we know is developed from something we have read, heard, or seen. Therefore, these other thoughts necessarily influence what we write. To the best of our knowledge, we have given specific credit where appropriate.

Rather than footnotes or references, we have listed the works that have provided significant information in one way or another, since this is often in concepts rather than quotes.

Statements that are attributed to us are things we have used commonly and do not recall seeing from someone else. Others obviously have similar thoughts. If we have made an oversight in any credits, we apologize and we would appreciate your comments.

1

WHAT IS YOUR BACKGROUND?

> Thought
> *Who is this God?*
> *Good question!*
> *Think about it.*

What are you talking about ─────────────

How does the supernatural relate to people? Do you have curiosity and many questions about the supernatural? Do most books on the topics get too deep or too far out? Is there really a Creator or did the universe just happen? What are angels? Since the beginning of history, these questions have been the topics of theology and mythology.

Would you believe that the term God provokes some kind of thought in every person? Whether the person is atheist, agnostic, or believer, he or she has a reaction. Wait a second. What are those descriptions?

Many people do not even know where they fit in the spectrum of atheist to believer. An atheist is one who denies the existence of God. An agnostic is one who does not know if there is a God, and is not sure it can be known. A believer is convinced that there is a living God.

The challenge of most studies in theology is there are many terms, ideas, and concepts. These generally are not used in common, practical communications and language.

Our objective is to take the ideas from the religious realm, then transfer the thoughts to the thinking of everyday relationships. That may seem like a tall order for a topic that is often relegated to seminaries and monasteries.

After all, if there is a God, then that knowledge should be available to everyone. This work is intended for a very broad audience. It is a comprehensive interaction for the general audience inquisitive about other world issues. In addition, it provides a broad framework and has adequate detail for serious students. Moreover, the treatise is a comprehensive foundation for collegiate and seminarian studies.

Culture

Our discussion will be based on the traditions of Christians and Jews. The customs of these two cultural groups have impacted to some extent numerous other societies. Their practices represent a large part of the world religions. The principles are the predominant philosophy and foundation of Western civilization. Much of these traditions are brought to us through ancient writings. These manuscripts vary in style and language, but all unfold historical data and values.

First, we need a little information about the growth of these cultures and the associated languages. There are three basic language groups or cultures. The Western civilization is primarily based on the Indo-European, sometimes called Japhetic, language group. The Near and Middle East is primarily based on the Semitic language family. The deep African and Eastern societies are heavily dependent on the Hamitic language classification. The relationship between the various languages will be discussed in detail in later chapters.

The oldest, most popular religious writings are in Hebrew, the language of the Jewish people. The tongue is in the Semitic family.

This primary manuscript of the Jewish people has come to other cultures as the Old Testament of the Bible. The compilation by various writers dates back to approximately 1500 BC and the works were completed about 400 BC. In this literary masterpiece, only one short treatise, Daniel, was in another original language, Aramaic.

The next document also comes from the Jewish way of life, but it was written primarily in Greek. The anthology was penned during the height of the Roman Empire. While Latin was the government language, Greek was the educational and cultural language of the day.

The Greek language is in the Indo-European group. This work has come to other cultures as the New Testament of the Bible. The compilation by various writers was completed during approximately 60 years of the first century AD.

To keep from being repetitive and to provide more variety in reading, synonyms will often be used for the names of the Old and New Testaments. Alternative words for testament are covenant, record, writings, scripture, tribute, treatise, and anthology. The choice is somewhat dependent on the use of the reference.

Outside effect

These two combined records have provided the fundamental structure for a major part of the religions and cultures of the world. Many other groups, philosophies, and organizations have developed their own books from these references.

For example, the Islamic (Moslem) writings heavily refer to events and people recorded in those earlier seminal works. The writings by Mohammed were developed in Arabic about the seventh century. Another reference work was developed for the Mormons. Joseph Smith compiled it in English during the nineteenth century.

Although these peripheral writings will not be discussed, they do illustrate the broad influence of the Old and New Anthologies of early Jewish traditions.

Language ━━━━━━━━━━

The foundations of our Western thinking are these two primary documents, the Old and New Testaments of the Bible. To get some correlations of concepts, it will be necessary to refer to the original Hebrew and Greek words.

These are particularly beneficial for the English audience, since our language is very dynamic. With every living dialect, there are changes with time and usage. American English has changed substantially since the common King James dialect of 1611 AD. 'Thy' is no longer 'your' way of speaking.

A more recent example is the word sophisticate. For all history prior to a generation ago, it meant to render worthless by admixture or to adulterate. The word, just by repeated usage, has come to be associated with having acquired worldly knowledge or refinement.

Dr. James Strong compiled perhaps the most exhaustive correlation of Hebrew and Greek to English. The concordance, assembled in 1894, makes a study of every word in the original manuscripts.

The same word in the original was often translated in multiple ways. This was common to give a slightly different shade of meaning. To keep track of the original words, Strong arranged them alphabetically. He then assigned a simple, but ingenious, number to each word.

By tracking the numbers, it is possible to know the original word without being a linguistic scholar. Strong's numbers are shown in parenthesis, when referring to the original language. This will aid the student in verifying the linguistic translation.

Translation ────────────

When referring to the original writings, the words can be illustrated in three ways: original spelling, phonetic spelling, and conceptual meaning. Each has its merits in certain situations. All will be used in this treatise. Original spelling with the original letters is the most technically accurate, but difficult to comprehend. Phonetic spelling with modern letters is great for speaking. Conceptual meaning is the best source for comprehension.

By convention of the language, words that refer to names of specific people and locations are capitalized. Therefore, 'god' refers to any being with special attributes. In contrast, 'God' refers to the identity of the specific god of the Jewish and Christian religions. This similar practice of capitalization will be used for other names and references of God.

There is one other note of language differences. Many languages do not have articles such as 'a' and 'the' to designate a specific item. English uses modifiers 'a' or 'an' to refer to any item. English uses 'the' to identify a specific item of the same type. For example, 'a' book is any book, while 'the' book identifies a specific book from a collection. In languages without modifiers, it would simply be book.

Since the articles can be used to differentiate any item from a unique item, they appear in some ways to be related to the rules of capitalization. However, capitalization is used for a name while articles are used to distinguish which items.

When crossing between languages, there are three practices. Literal translation uses word substitutes that are as exact as possible. Conceptual translation uses ideas that are similar, but words that relate to the culture. Transliteration creates a new word in the language. It is similar in form, spelling, and sound to the original.

Let us start with an example of referring back to the original languages. Consider the English word theology. The term is a transliteration of two Greek words *theos* and *logos*. *Theos* is translated god or deity, while *logos* is translated study. Hence, theology is the study of a god or deity. It is apparent with only a little imagination, that the words are very similar.

Who is on first ────────────────

Any study should start at the beginning. Look at the ancient Hebrew writing called the Old Testament. The first book is named Genesis, which means the beginning. The first verse asserts the foundations of the manuscript.

> In the beginning, God created the heaven and the earth.
> - Genesis 1:1

What does this say and mean? What is the first prepositional phrase? When was that in relation to time? Who was there? Who was there before time? What action happened at time zero? What was the result of the action?

That single statement at the beginning of the Old Anthology is the summary of theology. One of the challenges of theology is to describe concepts and ideas that no one has seen. As an example, try to describe in words any person you know. Can you do it adequately that a stranger would be able to identify them?

The problem of adequate definition is compounded when many of the topics are abstract. Nevertheless, it is incumbent that individuals have some working knowledge of these ideas. This includes the relationship between God and man.

That is the purpose of our writing. By necessity, the discussion must be described in personal terms, which include our knowledge, understanding, and wisdom.

Guiding principles ────────────────

In the investigation of such a fantastic topic, a few focal points will provide guidance. The following passages will give you a brief glimpse of the subjects and topics about which you will be learning. These are just a peek at the spectrum of ideas across history.

An early military general, Joshua, was going through challenges. He had just taken command of a huge group of itinerant people in a desert of the Middle East. He recorded a promise to those that studied these principles.

> This word of the law shall not depart out of your mouth, but you shall meditate on it day and night, that you may observe to do according to all that is written in it. For then you shall make your way prosperous, and then you shall have great success.
> - Joshua 1:8

Several hundred years later, the country was consolidated by a single regent. Under King David, the nation was at its height of political power. David was noted as a military genius, lover of women, and great poet. It is recorded that he was a man after God's own heart, because of his respect for the Almighty. In one of his numerous songs, he recalled the power of that relationship in just a few words. The old word bless can also be rendered as praise or exalt.

> Bless the LORD, O my soul: and all that is within me, bless his holy name. Bless the LORD, O my soul, and forget not all his benefits:
> - Psalm 103:1-2

Many years later, an ancient Hebrew author, Jeremiah, was very distressed. He was known as the weeping prophet. He was delivering his vision during the last years of his nation's existence. The time was just before his country was overrun and exiled by a foreign government. He gave a concise view of the power of Deity.

> Ah Lord God! Behold, you have made the heaven and the earth, by your great power and outstretched arm. There is nothing too hard for you.
> - Jeremiah 32:17

Hundreds of years afterward, during the time of the Roman Empire, many nations were conquered. However, they were allowed to maintain their government and culture. This was in exchange for providing taxes and services to the Roman league of nations. During that era, new religious teaching arose from a most unusual Jewish scholar, Jesus of Nazareth. The last living member of this teacher's personal cadre of apostles was John. John wrote an intriguing description by his personal knowledge about this educator who has had more impact on culture than any other man in history.

> In the beginning was the Word, and the Word was with God, and the Word was God...
> And the Word was made flesh and dwelled among us.
> - John 1:1 & 14a

These passages are so descriptive of the topics to be researched. With that foundation, we are on to a phenomenal venture.

Review

Consider the following questions.

1. Where do you fit as an atheist, agnostic, or believer?
2. Which language was used for the earlier writings of the Old Testament?
3. The Western culture gets much of its thought process from which language?
4. In the 1611 AD English dialect, what is the word for your?
5. When referring to words in an original language, what are three ways to illustrate the word?
6. When translating from an original language, what are three practices for getting the meaning?

2

ICON, IMAGE, & LIKENESS

Thought
A 7 year-old boy's meaning of Bible:
Basic Information Before Leaving Earth

Back to basics ─────────────

The oldest recorded history that is still in common use is the Hebrew book called Genesis. This one work of art covers all the truth that is expanded in other books. The book is the foundation of all Apologetics for the Judeo-Christian religions. Only a brief word study of the first sentence gives a complete overview of theology. The one sentence declaration illustrates the vast spectrum of topics that are embodied in the entire manuscript.

The time record of the book of Genesis covers almost half of all human recorded history. There is always room for debate when estimating archaeological dates. Nevertheless, an early theologian, Ussher, calculated the first recorded date. It was estimated at 4004 BC. The record of Genesis ends with the Exodus, which occurred about 1500 BC.

Where did we come from? How did we get here? Are we just animals? Some argue the Bible is not a scientific document and therefore could not possibly answer these questions. That is only partially true.

Science by definition is the recording of observable, repeatable facts. However, neither creation nor human history is repeatable. Nevertheless, we can describe processes from the past based on information we gather. The record is very accurate when all data are observed. It has proven to be the longest lived, accepted, recorded history on the planet.

The first statement is a succinct declaration about origins.

> In the beginning, God created the heaven and the earth.
> - Genesis 1:1

The oldest and most revered reference declares God as the Creator. It establishes God was before time, in the beginning.

Man is an icon ━━━━━━━━━━━━━━━━

What is God like? We can only know by observing his likeness. However, what is his likeness? We begin to find clues in the beginning book of human history and theology.

An icon is an image or representation. We find the assertion that man as an icon or image is like the Creator. That should not be a great surprise. The imagery is declared then immediately reaffirmed.

> And God said, Let us make man in our image, after our likeness: and let them have dominion over the fish of the sea, and over the fowl of the air, and over the cattle, and over all the earth, and over every creeping thing that creeps upon the earth.
>
> So God created man in his own image, in the image of God created he him; male and female created he them.
> - Genesis 1:26 - 27

There are at least two observations from this encounter. First, mankind is a likeness of God. Second, as part of that image, mankind has dominion and control over the entire earth and all the critters on the earth. Dominion means command, dominance, power, and authority. In other words, the earth and the animals belong to man for his use.

The earth and all that is in it are for service and profit. Nevertheless, it should not be abused. It is the height of arrogance to think that man has the ability to ultimately destroy the earth or even a significant part. On the other extreme, it is simplistic to think that we are just a part of the earth and the animals are the same level and have as much rights as humans.

The principle was reaffirmed by the ancient King David millennia later.

> You made him to have dominion over the works of your hands; you have put all things under his feet:
> - Psalm 8:6

If the Creator made everything, then he has authority over all he made. Since man is like him, that power was explicitly transferred. Think about it. You have authority over all things to which you apply your mind.

Like who ━━━━━━━━━━━

There is much consternation among students about exactly what this likeness means. At the time of creation, mankind was created perfect, in the image of the Creator. Since a perfect Creator can only perform perfection, then the created human must be perfect initially. The Creation account explicitly declares that man, and angels, were originally created excellent.

> And God saw everything that he had made, and, behold it was very good.
> - Genesis 1:31

What is the implication of this logical observation? If there is imperfection, it necessarily came later because of some action by the created beings.

Beyond the implication that man was made in the image of God, this account provides many opportunities for discussion. First, the word for God is a plural form, but has singular application. It is used in a singular context with a singular verb. Second, God said 'us'. This clearly indicates there is a multiplicity.

In this multiplicity, there are three different identities cataloged in the creation account. First, God is acknowledged as the creator in the very first statement. Next, the Spirit of God hovered over the fluid morass in the second sentence. Finally, Yehovah God was embodied with the days of creation summarized in the next chapter of the book.

Most researchers throughout history have regarded this image to indicate a trinity. The term trinity is never used in any of the recorded passages of the Old or New Testaments. The concept is after the Greek term *trias* and Latin *trinitas,* which means simply a set of three things that form a unit. The equivalent non-religious word is triad.

Science accord ━━━━━━━━━━

My background is a scientist, engineer, researcher, author, technology entrepreneur, commercial pilot, university professor, and seminary dean. This experience creates other fields of study for correlations to theology. From years of research and education, a very simple principle has been observed. This has been reported in scientific literature. The basis of technical research is called the Triad Principle.

> Any item that can be uniquely identified can be further described by three members. - MOD

Universally in the physical sciences, we find this is a fundamental law. As a result, all uniquely defined, complete equations have three components.

Based on the triad principle of science, we can know or predict many things numerically. If anything is uniquely identified, then it is *one* item. A complete description of the one item would have *three* members.

When comparing aspects of the three members, two will appear to be very similar. In contrast, the third will seem perpendicular or very different.

God is in the details ━━━━━━━━━━

Pulling from previous math classes and learning of prime numbers, this one series of numbers has unique characteristics. They are not divisible by any other number. The sequence is 1, 2, 3, 5, 7, 11, 13, and continuing. Other than 2, all prime numbers are necessarily odd.

In relation, numbers that correlate to the Creator deity are always represented by the prime numbers. For example, unique items are represented by the number one. Each item has three members. The number seven represents completeness, such as the days of a week.

Other numbers tend to be associated with particular items. For example, six is often associated with human characteristics. Twelve is associated with leaders, such as the founding fathers of the Jewish culture and Arab culture, as well as the New Testament apostles. Forty is concerned with growth to a new level, such as the period of reign for the first kings, David and Solomon.

Pattern of analysis ━━━━━━━━━━

The principle of three members for one item is universal in physical science. Numerous illustrations, statements, and inferences indicate this idea. If the model is consistently correct through trials or experiments, then the hypothesis is valid. The result is a theory that describes a principle or law.

An example of this triad principle is seen through scientists performing extensive analysis into the states of water. Ice is the form that is solid and has fixed dimensions. Liquid is the common state at normal temperatures and can be controlled in an open container. Vapor is the gaseous state that is invisible, and fills any space, but is still very much water. In all states, the chemical molecule is still two hydrogen atoms and one oxygen atom. This is just one example of having three members of one item.

Time is another very intriguing concept. It is the measurement of a sequence of events. Some measurements are fixed. Some include time to give rate or speed. Others include a second time multiplier to give acceleration. The three times combined represent a triad. The solution of this relationship explains the decay of every natural system. In a later chapter, we will see how this has shown up in life expectancy.

There are an infinite number of illustrations of triads in nature. In all cases, the observation is only one item. However, it has three different members that describe various conditions of the one article.

The strongest evidence in the materials we are studying is the numerous illustrations of the trinity concept throughout the canon. The model of a three-member relationship will be used as the pattern of analysis for our study of theology. This provides a foundation and a framework for each category of items we investigate.

Away we go on the most fundamental, but encompassing adventure affecting mankind. What a fascinating topic.

Review ━━━━━━━━━━

1. What is an icon?
2. What is a triad?
3. What is the difference in a triad and trinity?
4 How many illustrations of a triad can you think of in nature?

3

CAN YOU COUNT TO THREE?

Thought
Steps to effective teaching
Learn - Do - Teach

Pattern ────────────────

The triad principle simply means any unique item will have three members existing simultaneously and inseparably. As conditions change, one may appear to dominate. Nevertheless, all still exist. The model has worked in the past and continues to be appropriate for every idea modern science has researched.

Humans are made, as we discussed previously, in the image of God. Then, if we determine the pattern of man, we have indications into the pattern of God. Using the term indications does not imply that man is equivalent, only that he is modeled after a particular form.

It is generally recognized in philosophy and theology studies that man responds in three ways, as a triad or trinity. The ideas and concepts used to describe these responses vary greatly, depending on the area of study. In philosophy, psychology, and physiology areas, the factors are called by technical, but common terms - emotional, physical, and mental or intellectual.

The identical elements were called by different terms 400 years ago. The 1611 AD manner of speaking was preserved in the most common English biblical translation. The rendition is called the Authorized Version or King James Version. Since this style has been used for so many years, the dialect has taken on religious overtones that were never intended.

Check the original language ──────────────

In many cases, words have become religious to the point that they are difficult to comprehend. Often, they have lost their basis in common language. The human factors are a prime example. The corresponding ideas in the older dialect are listed below.

Soul = Emotional
Body = Physical
Spirit = Mental

The Greek and Hebrew value of the words can be readily established from numerous manuscripts. The form may vary slightly depending on the usage in the sentence. Nevertheless, the common root is widely known.

The phonetic forms of the Greek words are commonly identified and used.

Psyche (5590)   = Emotional
Soma (4983)   = Physical
Pneuma (4151) = Mental

The Hebrew roots are also well known.

Nephesh (5315) = Emotional
Basar (1320)   = Physical
Ruwach (7307) = Mental

It should be noted that language reflects the culture and thought processes. In Greek philosophy, the three components could be discretely isolated into three individual entities. However, in Hebrew philosophy, the three identifiable factors were inseparable. The structure demanded there be a body to surround the soul and be a residence for the spirit.

The Western thought process has much of its foundations in Greek culture, while the Eastern process is more closely allied with Hebrew thinking. This issue of thought processes involving discrete versus inseparable is the starting point of many theological discussions which end up being called mysteries. They are enigmas primarily because of a difference in logic approach.

Retranslate ―――――――

Some very conservative lecturers may disagree with the premise that the words correspond. Take the Greek root words through current translation software. This will yield the present day value of the words. The current translation explanation corresponds precisely with the technical terms listed previously.

A reference used in most translations is the *Septuagint*. This Greek rendition of the Hebrew scripture was initially released about 250 BC. The original translation was done by 70 Jewish scholars. This led to the name, which is derived from the Latin for the word seventy. Hence, it is often represented by the Roman numerals for seventy, LXX. The first version was the Torah. Various later iterations have somewhat clouded the original work.

Nephesh (5315), the Hebrew root word for emotional, occurs 753 times in the ancient texts. The *Septuagint* renders the expression into the Greek articulation *psyche (5590)* about 600 times. The Authorized Version uses 28 different words to translate the idea into English. Of that number, 475 times it is portrayed as soul. Another 117 times it is life. Other renderings embrace person, heart, creature, will, desire, and appetite, among other things.

It is interesting that soul has religious connotations while psyche has just the opposite in current usage. Dr. Spiro Zodhiates has an excellent comment on understanding the word. "More than 400 times *nephesh* is translated as soul in English. This is unfortunate, because many people today are then forced to think of this noun in a metaphysical, theological sense."

The Hebrew word *ruwach (7307)* has been variously translated as mind, wind, and spirit. In one instance, it is rendered as in the cool. Refer to Genesis 3 where God was in the cool *(ruwach, 7307)* of the day.

The original ancient writings were composed in the vernacular language of the day. The manuscript was intended for everyday use, not necessarily as a religious essay. With that concept in mind, we will refer to the three relationships of a person in the current language usage rather than the esoteric religious sounding words.

Even the technical concepts have various shades of meaning. The nuances of a particular idea depend on the application. Some of the more common thoughts are associated with each factor.

Emotional: appetite, will, feelings, desires, drive, and dreams
Physical: action, response, and body motion
Mental: attitude, intellect, decision, logic, or reason

Location, location, location

Each of the perspectives correlates with a particular location relative to the body. Emotional is an internal characteristic that may not be apparent to others. Physical is the external appearance that others can see. Mental is the air or atmosphere that relates to a person and that is perceived on a different plane. It is reflected in the idea of sensing what someone is thinking.

Awareness of the factors is detected by the senses. Physical is represented by the five senses - touch, taste, see, smell, and hear. Emotional is called the sixth sense, sometimes referred to as intuition. It is a feeling about the rectitude of a situation. Mental may be the seventh sense. It is an air or sensation of completeness and wellness or the counterpoint.

Any one item, by definition, is a unique representation. Furthermore, there are many items. All of which have three members. This analytical subdivision continues as far in depth as an item is researched. As a result, there are myriad ways to describe any complex system made of unique items.

Mind over matter ━━━━━━━━━━━━

The brain is the mechanism that controls all the actions and factors of the body. The leading university level anatomy text by Gray segregates the brain into a complete suite of seven sections. The subdivisions are named from the spinal cord to the top. These are medulla oblongata, pons, cerebellum, midbrain, thalamus, hypothalamus, and cerebrum.

The segments are grouped into three areas, the hindbrain, midbrain, and forebrain, respectively. The hindbrain and midbrain coordinate the autonomous and reflex activity of the body. The functions include posture, muscle tone, and life functions.

The cerebrum is the top of the forebrain. It is the seat of learning, logic, and reasoning.

The back parts of the forebrain control the physiological response of the autonomous nervous system. Related activity is the biological clock and sexual behavior.

Emotions are largely controlled by the limbic system. Primary limbic components are parts of the thalamus, hypothalamus, and deep recesses of the forebrain. The limbic system contains a pleasure center and a punishment center.

When that body part is stimulated, there is an emotional feeling. The sensation may include hunger, pain, sexual desire, anger, and fear. In turn, coordinated physiological responses are initiated in the limbic system. The results may be increased heart rate, panting, blushing, or sweating.

The physiological reaction has caused emotions to be associated with the internal organs. In some circles, emotions are called the soul. This is also variously referred to as having a heart or guts.

Word pictures ━━━━━━━━━━

So, how does all this fit together? A diagram is beneficial. The standard model for a control system with feedback is shown.

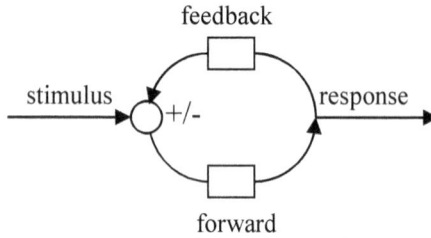

The diagram can be explained in just a few lines. A stimulus causes an emotion to move forward. The emotion promotes a physical response.

The mental state of mind analyzes the response and feedback controls the emotion. The control may be positive reinforcement, which causes the physical to grow. On the other hand, it may be a negative signal, which causes the physical effect to diminish to nothing.

When restated in 1611 AD dialect, the analysis sounds more religious. A provocation causes pride or anger to rise-up. The flesh reacts. The spirit causes a change of heart.

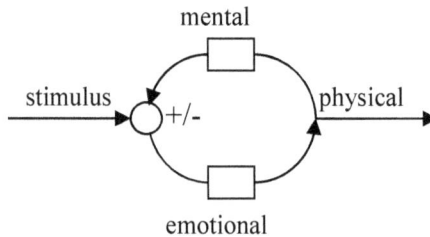

What about theology ─────────

What is the theological implication of this scientific discussion? We have just researched a model of how a man functions. Since man is in the image of the Creator, we have indications about his characteristics.

We can conclude that one facet of God is the triad relationship. He has a will or emotional identity. He can take on a body or physical person in time. He is a Spirit or intellectual member. All these exist simultaneously and are inseparable.

We talk with the Creator by our prayer thoughts. His Spirit in turn influences our spirit through the mind. Our mental faculties then control our heart or emotions.

Have you ever had a very close relationship with someone? You can sense their attitudes and what they are thinking. This is a similar principle.

This science discussion has three (obviously) key objectives. First, the triad model is valid for subsequent analyses of each topic we will address. Second, the concept is very comprehensible and can be explained in everyday terms, as well as religious. Third, this illustrates the Bible is applicable to all areas of our life, including the sciences.

Is it not fascinating that the Creator made man in his image? One result is man can communicate with his Creator. What an awesome God!

Contemplation ─────────

There are diverse circumstances that exist on the earth. The early scribe, John, counseled to check out the spirits.

> Beloved, believe not every spirit, but try the spirits whether they are of God: because many false prophets are gone out into the world.

- I John 4:1

You want to be around some people. Others you want to get away from as quickly as possible. People are influenced by the spirits.

In addition to the mental or spirit world, the emotions can also dramatically influence situations. For example, an emotionally angry person creates a strong feeling to avoid.

A little history

Our objective is to minimize religious terminology and to present *Who Is This God?* in current vernacular. Therefore, this section may be skipped with no loss of understanding. It is only provided to give a complete framework for the treatise.

The study and understanding of God has gone through a variety of interpretations throughout history. These have been heavily influenced by the culture of the time. Immediately after the completion of the writings of the New Testament, the interpretation was based on a relationship experience that served a function. As heresy began to develop, dogma was established to give rules of practice.

Theophilus of Antioch first applied the Greek term *trias*. The Latin *trinitas* was first used by Tertullian, a lawyer and presbyter in Carthage, before 220 AD. Tertullian taught the Son and Spirit are part of the one being of substance with the Father.

His writings challenged the heresy of modalism or Sabellianism, which teaches that the Father, Son and Spirit are sequentially the same, and the Son did not exist before the incarnation. Modalism was a distorted effort to preserve monotheism and to combat tritheism. The result is similar to a variation of Unitarian, which teaches there is only God, and Jesus is not God.

About 318 AD, Arius of Alexandria claimed that the Father was the only God and that the Father created the Son and the Son created the

Holy Spirit. As such, each was a separate being. To put down this Arian heresy was the stimulus for Constantine the emperor to call the ecumenical council of Nicea in 325 AD. The result was the Nicean Creed, which affirmed the divinity of the Son and Holy Spirit, but left intact the concept of separate beings.

Athanasius of Alexander participated in the Nicean Council. His writings during the next 50 years furthered the idea of the Godhead of three distinct individual persons who were all divine. Although heavily influenced by the Greek understanding, this dogma became the orthodox teaching of the Catholic Church. The Athanasian Creed was developed some years later and it seems to show influence of St. Augustine's writing.

The positions of Catholic, Protestant, and Independent churches can be traced to one of the various teachings of the first four centuries after the completion of the Scripture.

Over a century ago, the classical trinity of orthodox Christianity was concisely stated in the abstract of principles of the Southern Baptist Theological Seminary (Art. III). "God is revealed to us as Father, Son, and Holy Spirit, each with distinct personal attributes, but without division of nature, essence, or being."

With the acrimony associated with any religious teaching that may vary in some form from a perceived convention, any writer is subject to being labeled. That is unfortunate, since the earliest teachings were very much about relational understanding.

Although our theology is very obviously conservative Trinitarian, our approach is to make the concepts relatable to anyone. This necessarily can only be accomplished from a classical research analysis and going back to the source of first century practices that preceded religious dogma.

Specifically, we have found the word 'person' to be sometimes confusing for many people, since it can imply three separate mortals. This is particularly a problem when working with people from Eastern cultures. That is not surprising since three individuals is primarily a Greek concept, which strives to isolate discrete components. In contrast, the Eastern cultures see any such relationships as inseparable. We have worked with people from over 35 countries and found that one word is a stumbling point to meaningful dialogue about the God of the universe. It just does not translate well.

Moreover, the word is used only two times in the Authorized Version to refer to God. In both instances, it is a New Testament discussion of the physical person, Jesus.

Therefore, we will be judicious in our discussions to maintain accuracy, but will dispense with that particular term.

Numerous alternatives are illustrated throughout the canon. The legal scholar Paul in correspondence to Corinth provides a better example in a rather lengthy discourse. The introduction follows.

> For as the body is one, and has many members, and all the members of that one body, being many, are one body, so also is Christ.
> - I Corinthians 12:12

> The body is a unit, though it is made up of many parts; and though all its parts are many, they form one body. So it is with Christ.
> - I Corinthians 12:12 NIV

Review ——————

1. Describe a circumstance when you have entered an area and had a strong feeling about the situation.
2. Describe at least one environment that you saw which created an atmosphere of well-being.

CROSS-CULTURAL

Emotional	*Physical*	*Mental*	*Relationship*
soul	body	spirit	1611AD use
appetite	action	attitude	A words
psyche (5590)	*soma (4983)*	*pneuma (4151)*	Greek
nepesh (5315)	*basar (1320)*	*ruwach (7307)*	Hebrew

4

NAME THAT GOD

Thought
Our goal:
Elegantly simple

Pattern ━━━━━━━━━━━

There is substantial revelation of the different identities associated with the name of God. We will find, as we advance through various topics, that there is only one individual God. In varied circumstances, a person may relate in a way that is primarily emotional, physical, or intellectual. God is revealed and relates in a similar fashion.

A majority of one, God ━━━━━━━━━━━

The foundations are critical to any research. As such, we will return to the very first sentence in the anthology. The very first Hebrew word used to identify God is *Elohiym (430)*.

> In the beginning, God *(Elohiym)* created the heaven and the earth.
> - Genesis 1:1

The word is probably best translated almighty. It is used 2606 times in the Hebraic Old Testament. As noted earlier, this word has a plural form but it is used with singular verbs. That construction is compatible with the idea of three members of one God.

As no other word, this single term is recognized to define the Creator. The concept is the essence of all that is superior to mankind. Essence is another word used to describe the emotions or soul. That feature is the internal or inherent characteristic of an individual will.

Hovering, Spirit ━━━━━━━━━━

The next Semitic word associated with God is *ruwach (7306)*.

> ...And the Spirit *(Ruwach)* of God moved upon the face of the waters.
> - Genesis 1:2

The word occurs 378 times. Of those, 232 times it was translated Spirit in the Authorized Version accounting. In other frequent usage, it was translated wind in 92 cases. In 27 instances, it was rendered breath. In another place, it was called cool.

The air describes a situation that is unconstrained by physical description. When you enter a room, a certain air is associated with your first sensation. That air, atmosphere, or ambiance you sense is embodied in the concept of the word spirit. The characteristic is around an entity. That feature is associated with the mental faculties.

What is proper, Yehovah ━━━━━━━━━

The third word associated with God during the creation account is *Yehovah (3068)*.

> ...in the day that the LORD *(Yehovah)* God made the earth and the heavens.
> - Genesis 2:4

This is the proper name of the Creator. In ancient writings, some legalists considered the word too sacred to write or speak directly. It was applied euphemistically with only the four letters, without any vowel pointing. That construct is called a tetragrammaton. The letters are variously transliterated into English as *YHWH* or *JHVH*.

When vowels are applied to the tetragrammaton, we obtain Yahweh or Jehovah. These are exactly equivalent, representing only a slight difference in translation of pronunciation. In different languages, the letters 'Y' and 'J' may convert interchangeably because of articulation. Similarly, 'U', 'V', or 'W' may be exchanged. In other tongues, 'I' and 'J' are equivalent. Dr. Strong used a blend of letters that appears to be a better rendering, *Yehovah (3068)*.

When the Hebrew was translated into English in 1611, the editors opted to follow the ancient practices. Therefore, they did not use any indication this was a proper name. They simply translated the word as LORD, a four-letter symbolism. The entire word was capitalized to differentiate it from another word meaning the title Lord. This tradition has been carried over to many of the newer versions and revisions, even though it is an inadequate translation.

That choice is unfortunate on several accounts. First, when hearing, it is impossible to tell which concept of LORD *(Yehovah)* or Lord (Sir) is used. This makes it impossible to identify whether the word is a name or a title. As we progress in the investigation of *Who Is This God?*, we will find it desirable to make that distinction. A name is very personal, while a title is stilted and generic.

To assist in clarity of understanding during speaking discussions, we will use the transliterated term *Yehovah*. The word was applied 6519 times, far more than any other term or combination for the Deity. It is obvious that it is intended to be used. The very idea of a proper name indicates a personal God who is accessible to mankind.

The feature of this name is associated with the physical person of God.

What was that sir, Lord ——————————

An additional title that is linked to the Creator is *Adonay (136)*.

> And Abram said, Lord *(Adonay)* GOD *(Yehovah)*, what will you
> give me, seeing I go childless,
> - Genesis 15:2

The address was applied 434 times in the original manuscript. The title is closely associated with nobility or a peerage.

The term was brought into the English Bible by the British culture during the seventeenth century. That environment was heavily steeped in regal traditions. Hence, Lord was a very elegant title representing a proprietor, master, gentry, or other prestigious rank.

The title did not imply slavery on the part of the person using it. British citizens could not be treated as slaves or serfs since the thirteenth century.

It is more common to address a lord by the title Sir accompanied by his name. Lord is the title or rank. Sir is the personal address. The above reference for Lord God could be accurately rendered Sir *Yehovah*. This construction brings the relationship more intimate and current.

Note here a problem that is created with the translation practices. In their desire to avoid using *Yehovah*, the translators typically used the LORD construct. However, when used with *Adonay* (Lord), they were forced to stick in still another word. Therefore, God *(Elohiym)* was substituted for *Yehovah* to avoid using LORD. Otherwise, for consistency, the translation would have been Lord LORD. This choice of word usage ultimately destroys any personal comprehension of *Yehovah* in the message.

The title lord is also associated with a husband. This usage is consistent since it indicates protector and provider. Shortly after the above reference to Lord, Sarah used the same term for Abraham, her spouse.

> Therefore Sarah laughed within herself, saying, after I am waxed old shall I have pleasure, my lord being old also?
> - Genesis 18:2

What is in a name ▬▬▬▬▬▬▬

We can learn a great deal by observing the traditions of a name. Shem is an excellent example. Shem is the Hebrew translation for name. As one of Noah's three sons, he was a survivor of the universal flood that virtually destroyed the planet. Moreover, he is the ancestor of all Semitic people. As such, his moniker could reasonably be expected to represent all names in that culture.

Adam is another fascinating example. Adam is the Hebrew noun for mankind and ruddy. As the first person, it is expected that his name would come to represent the entire human race.

A later chapter will deal with the genealogy of the early human family, including these two gentlemen.

Associations ▬▬▬▬▬▬▬

Different perspectives of the supreme deity are associated with various situations. Look at the first six chapters of Genesis to find the pattern for forms of the name used throughout history.

God *(Elohiym)* is when the supreme entity is implied and elevated away from humans. LORD *(Yehovah)* is personal when there is discussion with a human. Lord *(Adonay)* is used frequently in negotiations of a family or business type situation.

God *(Elohiym)* is primarily presented during the creation account. *Yehovah* God is predominant with Adam and Eve. *Yehovah* then becomes the leading representation. It appears that the proper or individual name became more common when the people accepted a personal relationship. The change in relationship is explicitly declared.

...then began men to call upon the name of the LORD *(Yehovah).*
- Genesis 4:26

The Spirit was the primary entity in attitude and reasoning about moral issues.

...My Spirt shall not always strive with man,
- Genesis 6:3

Names that we use reflect our relationships. In some cases we expect formal addresses while in others we use very casual terms of endearment. The same is reflected in interactions with Deity. Variations of these names will be looked at in the next chapter.

Review

1. What are the English and Hebrew for the first identity of the Creator?
2. What are the English and Hebrew for the wind characteristic of God?
3. What are the English and Hebrew for the proper name of the personal God?
4. What are the English and Hebrew for the title associated with the personal God?

NAMES

Emotional	Physical	Mental	Relationship
God	LORD	Spirit	member
Elohiym	*Yehovah*	*Ruwach*	Hebrew
almighty	personal name	breath, air	translation

5

NICKNAMES, COMBOS, & SPECIALS

Thought
*If you are going to sell,
sell to people that buy.*
J. Stovall

Names mean things ──────────

Given names are often derived to describe a circumstance or situation. Do you know the meaning and the language etymology for your name? How closely does the meaning of your name relate to your personality? It is fascinating how our names reflect who we are.

There is an interesting play on words with some names. Joshua or *Jehosua (3091)* is a Semitic man's name meaning Jehovah *(Yehovah)* is salvation or liberation. When brought into Greek and the Romance languages, the Hebrew name becomes *Jesus (2424)*. What an interesting turn of events for *Yehovah*.

The two primary descriptions or names of the Supreme Deity are occasionally shortened or abbreviated. *Elohiym* commonly becomes *El* particularly when joined to a modifier. The abbreviation and its derivatives are frequently associated with family names in the Middle East. Similarly, *Yehovah* becomes *Yah (Jah)* when combined into expressions such as hallelujah.

41

El combo ─────────────

Three compounds are derived from the abbreviation of God *(El)*. Remember, three is the number associated with a complete scientific observation of a triad or trinity.

El elyon (5945) is most high God *(410)*.

> Melchizedek king of Salem brought forth bread and wine: and he was the priest of the most high *(elyon)* God *(El)*.
> - Genesis 14:18

This compound emphasizes the supremacy of the Creator above all other gods. The next sentence declares he is possessor of heaven and earth. This appears to be the spirit or intellectual entity.

Melchizedek is an interesting character himself. He was a priest and received tithes from Abraham. He is affirmed to be without father or mother. Tradition indicates he was Shem, a flood survivor and the father of the Semitic people. His heritage is discussed extensively in another chapter. Much later in time, the person of Jesus was called a priest after the order of Melchizedek.

El Shaddai (7706) is Almighty God *(410)*.

> And when Abram was ninety-nine years old, the LORD *(Yehovah)* appeared to Abram, and said unto him, I am the Almighty *(Shaddai, 7706)* God *(El, 410)*; walk before me,
> - Genesis 17:1

Shaddai probably is related to mountain, hence the mighty concept. Some scholars relate it to covenant keeping. The idea was used when the covenant with Abraham was reiterated. Abraham was named Abram at birth, but his name was changed when he became the father of many people. This name of God refers explicitly to a physical person.

El olam (5769) is everlasting God *(410)*.

And Abraham planted a grove in Beersheba, and called there on the name of the LORD *(Yehovah)*, the everlasting *(olam, 5769)* God *(El, 410)*.
- Genesis 21:33

Have you not heard, that the everlasting *(olam, 5769)* God *(El, 410)*, the LORD *(Yehovah)*, the Creator of the ends of the earth, faints not, neither is weary?
- Isaiah 40:28

The idea of everlasting is otherwise rendered perpetual, ancient, or all-inclusive. This stresses the absence of time. This is the emotional will.

Yehovah combo

Nine compounds or combinations are associated with the proper name *Yehovah*. These are variously called names, descriptions, or monuments of God. In either case, they tell more about *Who Is This God?*

Yehovah-jireh (3070) is Yehovah will provide.

Abraham called the name of that place Jehovahjireh: as it is said to this day, in the mount of the LORD it shall be seen.
- Genesis 22:14

Yehovah-nissi (3071) becomes Yehovah our protector.

Moses built an altar, and called the name of it Jehovahnissi: For he said, Because the LORD has sworn…
- Exodus 17:15

Yehovah-qadash (6942) turns into Yehovah your sanctifier.

…that you may know that I am the LORD that does sanctify you.
- Exodus 31:13

Yehovah-shalom (3073) converts to Yehovah is peace.

Peace be unto you; fear not: you shall not die. Then Gideon built an altar there unto the LORD, and called it Jehovahshalom:
- Judges 6:24

Yehovah-sabbaoth (6635) develops as Yehovah of hosts.

This man went up out of his city yearly to worship and to sacrifice unto the LORD of hosts in Shiloh.
- 1 Samuel 1:3

Yehovah-tsidkenu (3072) changes to Yehovah our righteousness.

In his days Judah shall be saved, and Israel shall dwell safely: and this is his name whereby he shall be called, the LORD our righteousness.
- Jeremiah 23:6

Yehovah-roi (7462) expands to Yehovah my shepherd.

The LORD is my shepherd; I shall not want.
- Psalms 23:1

Yehovah-shammah (3074) transpires as Yehovah is there.

...and the name of the city from that day shall be, The LORD is there.
- Ezekiel 48:35

Yehovah elohiym Israel (3478) transfers to Yehovah God of Israel.

I will sing praise to the LORD God of Israel.
- Judges 5:3

...four or five in the outmost fruitful branches thereof, says the LORD God of Israel.
- Isaiah 17:6

I Am

The Creator in his back-to-back discussion with Moses applies a unique name to himself. He simply called himself, I Am.

And God *(Elohym)* said unto Moses, I AM WHO I AM: and he
said, Thus shall you say unto the children of Israel, I AM *(1961)* has
sent me unto you.
- Exodus 3:14

There are many times this term is used throughout the canon. The
Old Testament uses the Hebrew 75 times while the New Testament
records the Greek I Am 146 times.

I Am seems to simply mean I exist. That declaration carries many
implications. The obvious one is without time or ongoing. I Am
covers the past, present, and future.

With us ——————

One of the most significant combinations with the abbreviation *El*
occurs in a prophecy. An ancient philosopher, Isaiah, had
confidence enough to record a prediction. It was approximately 742
years before the forecast was achieved.

Behold, a virgin shall conceive, and bear a son, and shall call his
name Immanuel *(6005)*.
- Isaiah 7:14

Immanuel is a transliteration of the Hebrew that literally is 'in man
God'. The term is a combination that simply announces that God is
with us. The anticipation revealed that God would come in a
physical person as a man. This foresight was satisfied with the
extraordinary birth of the man Jesus.

As stated in the prediction, the mother would be a virgin. In
combination with specific declarations by the tax collector,
Matthew, virgin asserts no sexual contact. Then how was the child
fathered? The name Immanuel explains that the father was God. The
public official, Matthew, further enlightens that the particular
member involved was the Spirit.

This circumstance of a deified birth has never been documented before or since that time. The birth to the virgin was a unique event in human history.

The proclamation Immanuel is valid to this day. Since understand that the Spirit or mental relationship is very active, we can still say that God is with us.

The concepts

What a huge concept. The various names associated with God reveal a tremendous amount of information. The first three used during creation disclose the three relationships for the image of mankind. In addition, the title shows the nobility of God.

Three compounds with *El* exemplify the three perspectives of a man. However, compounds of *Yehovah* illustrate the personal relationship with mankind.

Can you think of a greater picture of *Who Is This God?*

Review

To better relate the addresses given to the supreme deity, list the following items associated with Deity:

1. What three names were associated during creation?
2. What is the title?
3. What are three combinations with the abbreviation or family name?
4. Give any three of the compounds with *Yehovah.*
5. What is the meaning of I Am?
6. What is the meaning of Immanuel?
7. Give a praise term with the abbreviation of *Yehovah.*

6

ATTRIBUTES ARE THE ULTIMATE

Thought
Surpass yourself.
Dr. Eden Ryl

Structure ━━━━━━━━━━━━

First, what is an attribute? This quality, trait, characteristic, or feature describes something. Attributes of deity are described by ideals.

The attributes of the Creator are most obvious when related to common concepts. Various writers have listed many attributes. Seldom do the lists match. They seem to reflect the preferences of the author.

For a God that creates, there should be a consistent pattern. Rather than memorize terms, we propose to look at a more structured understanding. The attributes are separated into categories of philosophy, science, and personality. Each category has three individual components. These components are common concepts within each of the fields of study.

By definition, God is greater than all things. Therefore, when proper concepts are extended to their logical conclusion, they describe one of the attributes of the Creator.

PHILOSOPHY
Philosophy category ─────────

Philosophy covers all learning outside of technical precepts and practical arts. It includes all university training except medicine, law, and theology. At its core are logic, aesthetics, ethics, and metaphysics with reference to validity and limits.

Mathematics is the philosophy of using symbols and numbers to represent real objects and values. We will not discuss calculations or equations. Rather we will look at the symbols and concepts. The symbols allow very complex concepts to be described concisely.

Philosophy is constrained by three points. There is a starting point, base, or origin; an ending point, extreme, or limit; and the value point, reference, or measure. The logical conclusion of each of these points is an attribute of the Creator.

Perfect ─────────

The base or starting point is perfection, by definition. Starting with less than perfection would necessarily include starting with error. The word derives from the Latin *perfectus*. Perfect literally means excellent, finished, complete, or precise.

The logical extension of perfection is law or structure. Therefore, the base or starting attribute of the Creator is perfect and becomes law.

> The law of the LORD *(Yehovah)* is perfect...
> - Psalms 19:7

All natural laws come from perfection. A law is simply a statement of how something works. It is not an explanation of the consequences.

Laws have consequences, which lead to stability. Natural laws have perfect results. If you violate a law, you will have consequences.

Consequences are not the law, but the rejection of the law or rule. The results may vary, but the consequences are always the same.

If you violate the law of gravity, consequently you will hit the ground. It may be tripping, or it may be falling from a building. A person is not condemned to fall. Nevertheless, if he rejects the natural law, he will pay.

This attribute lets God be perfect in love. Consequently, when a person rejects that love, he will pay with eternal separation. He is not arbitrarily condemned to separation. It is a choice.

> As for God, his way is perfect; the word of the LORD *(Yehovah)* is flawless.
> - Psalms 18:30 NIV

> Be you therefore perfect (excellent), even as your Father, which is in heaven, is perfect (excellent).
> - Matthew 5:48

The last passage was declared by the God-man, Jesus. Father asserts that God is our progenitor. We are here because of him and his creative acts.

Is it possible for a person to be perfect? Can a person pursue excellence?

Unique

The value of a point is unique. Unique implies exceptional, single, exclusive, set apart, or distinctive. Therefore, the reference or measurement attribute of the Creator is exceptional or unique.

In religious terms, this is often called holy. Our goal is to keep concepts applicable for every person in every day life. Therefore, our objective is to be like God, which is to be exceptional.

> ...Be holy (exceptional), because I am holy (exceptional).
> - Leviticus 11:45, I Peter 1:16

Unique also carries the idea of single or only one. That definitely is an attribute of the Creator. Another unique attribute is there can only be one that creates a particular thing.

> It will be a unique day, without daytime or nighttime - a day known to the LORD *(Yehovah)*.
> - Zechariah 14:7 NIV

Infinite ───────────────

The extreme or end point is at infinity. Infinite implies exceeding, vast, immense, forever or everything. Other explanations are extending beyond, lying beyond, or greater than any limit.

The word meaning is so expansive, that it is very difficult to define with strictly positive concepts. In fact, the word itself derives from the Latin *in + finitus*. This literally means not finite or measurable.

The logical extension of infinite is beyond measure. Therefore, the extreme attribute of the Creator is best stated as infinite.

In traditional religious terms, this is often called omnipotent. That term carries the idea of all power. Humans are not encouraged to be infinite or all powerful, since this logically is not possible.

> Great is our Lord *(Yehovah)*, and of great power: his understanding is infinite.
> - Psalms 147:5

> ...with God all things are possible.
> - Matthew 19:26

> Ah Lord God *(Yehovah)*! behold, you have made the heaven and the earth by your great power and stretched out arm, and there is nothing too hard for you:
> - Jeremiah 32:17

Fun with numbers ━━━━━━━━━

The topic of philosophy lends itself so beautifully to numbers and symbols applications. By no stretch of the imagination, will this be a mathematical analysis.

Perfect (excellent) is the base or starting point, represented by the number zero (0). This value is the lower limit or foundation of numbers. The symbol is very symmetrical, with no abrupt direction changes. Alone, it has no value. However, as a placeholder, zero makes other numbers an order of magnitude greater. One becomes ten, ten becomes one hundred, all because of the zero.

Unique (exceptional) is the reference or value point, obviously represented by the number one (1). Any value can be obtained by adding enough ones together. It is the most powerful of all numbers.

Infinite (exceeding) is the extreme or ending point, represented by a very unusual symbol (∞). The symbol is the upper limit of numbers. This symbol is without beginning or end. Regardless of direction of travel along the path, you will ultimately end up at the same place. It continues forever.

SCIENCE
Science category ━━━━━━━━━

The next attribute category is science. Science simply means knowing. Science is observing repeatable events, then developing an explanation. If the events are not repeatable and observable, the study is a hypothesis or conjecture.

All physical science can be defined by three measurements - matter, time, and space. Each of these also is three faceted. The logical conclusion of these measurements is the attribute of the Creator.

Stable ━━━━━━━━━

Matter is the stuff that the five senses can detect. Matter is the item that gives characteristics. The three unique characteristics of matter are mass, charge, and magnetism.

Matter implies things exist. Stable is unchanging, consistent, steady, or firm. If something exists in all conditions, the logical conclusion is it must be stable. Therefore, the matter attribute of the Creator is stable.

In religious terms, this is often called immutable. That is a very long synonym for stable.

> ...with whom is no variableness, neither shadow of turning.
> - James 1:6

The next reference precedes a discussion of giving tithes and offerings instead of robbing God.

> For I am the LORD *(Yehovah)*, I change not;
> - Malachi 3:6

We are directed to have this stable attribute.

> But let him ask in faith, nothing wavering. For he that wavers is like a wave of the sea driven with the wind and tossed.
> - James 1:6

Perpetual ━━━━━━━━━

Time is the measurement of a sequence of events. There are three characterizations of time. Some measurements are independent of time. Some include time. Others include a second time multiplier.

Time implies a definite interval or period when things happen. If something exists during all the time characterizations, the logical conclusion is it must be perpetual. Therefore, the time attribute of the Creator is that he is perpetual.

In religious terms, this is often called eternal or everlasting.

> Before the mountains were brought forth, or ever you had formed
> the earth and the world, even from everlasting to everlasting, you
> are God.
> - Psalms 90:2

> I am God, and there is none like me, declaring the end from the
> beginning, and from ancient times the things that are not yet done...
> - Isaiah 46:10

> ...a perpetual incense before the LORD *(Yehovah)* throughout your
> generations.
> - Exodus 30:8

Any physical item is constrained to exist in time. Since God
supercedes time, he is not constrained to a physical body.
Nevertheless, he can move into time and take on the physical form.

Everywhere ───────────

Space is the measurement by distance. Space is often rendered as
heaven in the ancient Hebrew and Greek manuscripts.

There are three types of space measurement. The most common is
three-dimensional space that gives volume to matter. The second is
the force distance measurement that creates energy. The third is the
motion measurement that gives direction and creates fields.

Three-dimensional space has three regions. The closest is the area
we occupy and the air we breathe. Next is the region of birds,
airplanes, and weather. Outer space is the region of celestial bodies
such as the moon, sun, and stars.

In metaphysical context, space includes three realms. The natural
realm is the abode of humans. The supernatural realm is the place of
the spirit world. The ultra-natural realm is the space of God that
cannot be penetrated.

Space implies a definite region where things happen. If something is simultaneously located in all regions, then it is ubiquitous or everywhere. Therefore, the space attribute of the Creator is everywhere.

In religious terms, this attribute is often called omnipresent.

> If I ascend up into heaven, you are there: if I make my bed in hell, behold, you are there. If I take the wings of the morning, and dwell in the uttermost parts of the sea; Even there shall your hand lead me, and your right hand shall hold me.
> - Psalms 139:8-10

> But will God indeed dwell on the earth? Behold, the heaven and heaven of heavens cannot contain you; how much less this house that I have built?
> - I Kings 8:27

> Do not I fill heaven and earth? says the LORD *(Yehovah)*.
> - Jeremiah 23:24

PERSONALITY
Personality category ——————————

The next attribute category is personality or behavior. Personality is the image of humans that is like the Creator. An earlier discussion, investigated image concepts extensively. This discussion will simply determine the attribute that relates to each factor.

Personality is defined by three relationships - emotional, physical, and mental. The logical extent of these behavioral traits is the attribute of the Creator.

Absolute ——————————

Emotion is variously related to will, appetite, feelings, desires, drive, and conscious dreams. It is the most intimate of the personality features.

Emotion implies there is a will or desire for something. The logical conclusion is that it must be absolute will. Therefore, the emotional attribute of the Creator is absolute.

In religious terms, this is often called sovereign. That is an excellent term, since it is regal with the authority of a king. However, even a monarch's authority is restricted compared to absolute power.

As is obvious, emotions including will are one of the aspects given to mankind. How does the absolute will of God interact with the free will of humans?

In his absolute will, he has allocated certain decisions to people. A person's will is simply to take advantage of or to reject natural laws. The rejection of the laws, as we discussed earlier, has consequences.

We do not have willpower to change natural laws. Natural laws are the result of the perfect attribute, and we are not perfect in this life.

Within our allotted freedom, we are allowed to make our choices, even if they are detrimental. This is obvious in the following reference.

> The Lord is…not willing that any should perish, but that all should come to repentance.
> - II Peter 3:9

The will of God is most substantiated in his creation and control of natural order.

> But our God is in the heavens: he has done whatsoever he has pleased.
> - Psalms 115:3

> Of his own will he produced us with the word of truth,
> - James 1:18

> You are worthy, O Lord, to receive glory and honor and power: for you have created all things, and for your pleasure they are and were created.

- Revelation 4:11

We ultimately have access to the absolute will of Yehovah through the name of Jesus. This is a commitment, and a perfect, infinite, stable God can only make true statements.

If you shall ask any thing in my name, I will do it.
- John 14:14

Self-sufficient ━━━━━━━━━

Physical relates to action, response, and body motion. It is the most visible of the personality features.

Physical implies a body for some activity. If there is a body, the logical extent is it must be self-sufficient. Therefore, the physical attribute of the Creator is self-sufficient.

In religious terms, this is often called self-existent.

For from him, and through him, and to him are all things.
- Romans 11:36

For as the Father has life in himself; so has he given to the Son to have life in himself;
- John 5:26

And he is before all things, and by him all things consist (stay together).
- Colossians 1:17

All-knowing ━━━━━━━━━

Mental includes attitude, intellect, decision, logic, or reason. The personality feature reaches across space.

Mental implies intellect. If someone has intellect, then the logical extreme would be all knowing. Therefore, the mental attribute of the

Creator is all knowing. In religious terms, this is often called omniscience.

> O the depth of the riches both of the wisdom and knowledge of God! How unsearchable are his judgments, and his ways past finding out!
> - Romans 11:33

> ...because greater is he that is in you, than he that is in the world.
> - I John 4:4

What does it all mean ⸻

Attribute describes a unique quality, trait, characteristic, or feature. Rather than memorize terms, we have used a structured approach.

Separate the attributes into categories of philosophy, science, and personality. Each category has three individual components. These components are common concepts in each of the fields of study. The supreme or extreme depiction for the components is the deified attribute.

In philosophy, we can be excellent and exceptional; but we have bounds so we are finite. In personality, we have the emotional, physical, and mental relationships, but less than the extent of the Creator. In science, we exist in matter, space, and time. So we can be stable, however, we are excluded from perpetual and everywhere.

Review ⸻

Identify the following relationships associated with attributes.

1. Which three attributes of God are also available to mankind?
2. God is perfect, what is the equivalent attribute for a person?
3. God is unique, what is the equivalent attribute for a person?
4. God is stable, what is the equivalent attribute for a person?
5. What is the attribute of time associated with God?
6. From what attribute is law derived?

7. As a result of law, what is the gift given to mankind?

ATTRIBUTES

1	2	3	Relationship
base	*value*	*extreme*	philosophy
perfect/excellent	unique/exceptional	infinite	current
law	holy	omnipotent	traditional
matter	*time*	*space*	science
stable/consistent	perpetual	everywhere	current
immutable	eternal	omnipresent	traditional
emotional	*physical*	*mental*	personality
absolute	self-sufficient	all-knowing	current
sovereign	self-existent	omniscient	traditional

7

WHAT A CHARACTER

Society needs ───────────────

Character is a group of mental, moral, and ethical traits that describe a person and society. Character is how a person behaves when no one is looking.

If a culture is going to survive, society has certain expectations and requirements of its citizens. Some features are universal, such as the protection of life. Others are preferences, such as hairstyle. Character is the trait that promotes equitable treatment of every person, regardless of station.

The behavior of a person is determined by the nature of his dealings. He has three responses - personal, interpersonal, and deity. Personal is with himself, interpersonal is with others, and deity is with the higher power. Alternately, the relationships are respectively called internal, horizontal or external, and vertical. These can easily correlate to the personality relationships of emotional, physical, and mental.

Where from ─────────

The list of character traits that are generally accepted is actually quite limited. In the Judeo-Christian ethical structure, these are identified in the historical and religious teachings. One brief and one comprehensive list have survived over two thousand years. That is a strong commendation of the value of the qualities.

Both lists are referred to as the fruit of the Spirit. Fruit is one of the products of a live organism. Fruit carries all the characteristics of the parent in the seed. Therefore, the character of God can be inferred from the compilation of both the short and comprehensive lists of the fruit of the Spirit.

> For the fruit of the Spirit is in all goodness, righteousness, and truth.
> - Ephesians 5:9
>
> But the fruit of the Spirit is love, joy, peace, patience, kindness, goodness, faithfulness, gentleness, self-control: against such there is no law.
> - Galatians 5:22-23 NIV

Each character trait will be investigated individually. Some of these expressions are from language usage seldom seen in every day communication, because of the age of the writings. As we discussed, the original language is Greek and was translated into archaic English 400 years ago.

To aid in comprehension, terms that are more familiar are associated with the ideas. The synonyms are used strictly to improve understanding. In no way are they intended to diminish the strength of the original concepts.

Personal application ─────────

All these values are considered positive attitudes in the human perspective. They are fruit; therefore, the characteristics are available to mankind. Since they are products of the Spirit, they come to people as mental attitudes. Nevertheless, they may be observed in different ways.

A person may embrace the trait within himself, such as being moral. Alternately, he or she may extend it to other people, such as treating others well. Moreover, other people will observe it in you.

In some circles, theology and religion are regarded as a private matter. That is impossible. What you think, feel, and act impacts others. Theology is very much about relationships.

There are terms for each of the traits that are personalized. Many authors use the internalized idea for the traits. However, we want to focus on the application for you and me. Therefore, the shade of meaning used for each trait will be the one that others observe in you.

Remember these are the character of God. Therefore, they are the highest of values. The short list is investigated first.

> For the fruit of the Spirit is in all goodness, righteousness, and truth.
> - Ephesians 5:9

Virtue ━━━━━━━━━━━━

Goodness *(agathosune, 19)* is one of two classes of goodness - passive and active. This is the energized or active goodness. The other class will be discussed in the next chapter. The idea is only translated goodness on four occasions. Alternative interpretations are virtue, worthwhile, well doing, and benefit.

Virtue is an excellent word, but in some circles has come to be primarily associated with chastity. Worthwhile has broader application and acceptance in current usage. The relationship is horizontal or with other people, since it is how others are treated.

> Now know I that the LORD *(Yehovah)* will do me good *(19)*...
> - Judges 17:13

For so is the will of God, that with well doing *(19)* you may put to silence the ignorance of foolish men:
- 1 Peter 2:15

Morality ─────────────

Righteousness *(dikaiosune, 1343)* is one of those concepts that have taken religious overtones. The term is seldom applied to humans and is often dropped from application discussions. To most people it is associated primarily with deity. In many cases, it is rendered just, right, freed, judgment, and justification. The word comes from a concept meaning tendencies and simply means right thinking.

Morality, honesty, justice, equity, fairness, impartiality, and lawfulness are renderings that are more familiar. The relationship is internal or focused on you personally.

> Righteous *(1343)* are you, O LORD *(Yehovah)*, and upright are your judgments.
> - Psalm 119:137

Perhaps one of the most profitable promises in the entire manuscript is based on pursuing the moral trait. Jesus himself declared it.

> But seek you first the kingdom of God, and his righteousness *(1343)*; and all these things shall be added unto you.
> - Matthew 6:33

In current vernacular, the verse is less stilted.

> But seek you first the realm of God, and his tendencies; and all these things shall be yours.

Integrity ─────────────

Truth *(alethia, 225)* has come to mean just the blunt facts. The word is variously translated as indeed, verity, surely, grinding, and very.

Truth is a legal term that can be used to distort intentions and reality. We have seen politicians that technically, within the law, tell the truth. However, they do not state accurate events or information. Therefore, they are telling the truth while distorting the circumstance and reality.

Integrity is a better rendering for our present usage. Integrity involves the facts, but tempered with judgment. It carries with it the idea of truth in concert with intentions.

My wife has a very personal illustration of integrity. The fact is a person (me) has a loss of hair. Integrity is saying nothing about it. Everyone understands the facts and the intent.

The relationship is vertical or how we deal with our maker. Integrity is illustrated in both the Old and the New Covenant.

> God is not a man, that he should lie; neither the son of man, that he should repent. Has he said, and shall he not do it? Or has he spoken, and shall he not make it good?
> - Numbers 23:19

> Jesus said unto him, I am the way, the truth *(225)*, and the life: no man comes unto the Father, but by me.
> - John 14:6

The character traits from the short list of the fruit are found in a letter to the people at Ephesus. These are an overview or summary of the complete list of traits, which will be investigated in the next chapter. Since the traits are the product of the Creator, they are designed for human consumption.

Review ────────────

1. Do these three traits effectively summarize what you desire to see in other people?
2. How do they fit you?

CHARACTER

Internal	Horizontal	Vertical	Relationship
emotional	physical	mental	perspective
morality	virtue	integrity	current use
right thinking	goodness	truth	Ephesians 5

8

MORE CHARACTER

Thought
Confidence -
the mental assurance that something is true.
MOD

Expanding an idea ━━━━━━━━━

The earlier three traits in the short list of the fruit of the spirit were recorded in a letter to the folks at Ephesus. Only one term is common with the more detailed accounting of the Galatians letter.

But the fruit of the Spirit is love, joy, peace, patience, kindness, goodness, faithfulness, gentleness, self-control: against such there is no law.
- Galatians 5:22-23 NIV

This comprehensive inventory is arranged very symmetrically. The first three items are internal, personal, or emotional concepts. The next three are horizontal, interpersonal, or physical notions. The third group is vertical, deity, or mental perceptions.

INTERNAL
Compassion ━━━━━━━━━

```
+INTERNAL+
compassion
charisma
calm

HORIZONTAL

VERTICAL
```

Love *(agape, 26)* is only one of three expressions translated into the same word. The following

65

three terms are sometimes referred to as love. Compassion *(agape, 26)* is emotional concern for others with a desire to give or help them. Erotic *(eros)* is physical, intimate, sexual attraction of one person for another. This form of love is only used in the Old Testament, so it does not have a Greek number. Friendship *(phileo, 5368)* is the mental appreciation for something, but lacks commitment.

The greatest compassion is shown in the most well known verse on the planet.

> For God so loved *(26)* the world, that he gave his only begotten Son, that whosoever believes in him should not perish, but have everlasting life.
> - John 3:16

The erotic love has no reference in the New Record. However, erotic stamina is declared in an older passage. This is from an equivalent Hebrew word *(ohab, 159)*. The passion of a one-night stand is in no way similar to the compassion of an enduring relationship.

> Come, let us take our fill of love until the morning: let us solace ourselves with loves *(ohab, 159)*.
> - Proverbs 7:18

The more casual friendship lacks the physical or emotional intimacy. In many cases, this concept is related to the word like. The first passage could easily have the word like substituted for love. In the second incident, Jesus made the address to his friend Judas, while he was being betrayed. The same root word is used for love and friend in all three examples.

> And love *(5368)* the uppermost rooms at feasts, and the chief seats in the synagogues...
> - Matthew 23:6

> And Jesus said unto him, Friend *(5368)*, why are you come?
> - Matthew 26:50

...whosoever therefore will be a friend *(5368)* of the world is the enemy of God.
- James 4:4

Charisma ──────────────

Joy *(chara, 5479)* is a crisp word representing gladness, hail, greeting, or exuberance. It has kept its traditional value. In addition, it has very fascinating derivatives seen below.

Well done, you good and faithful servant: you have been faithful over a few things, I will make you ruler over many things: enter you into the joy *(5479)* of your lord.
- Matthew 25:21

Grace *(charis, 5485)* is derived from the word *chara* and literally means joy, favor, gratitude, thanks, or pleasure. The idea is shown in a term applied to debts. A grace period is an extension, which is granted as a favor, to allow payment of the bill.

And the angel said unto her, Fear not, Mary: for you have found favor *(5485)* with God.
- Luke 1:30

And the child grew, and waxed strong in spirit, filled with wisdom: and the grace *(5485)* of God was upon him.
- Luke 2:40

For if you love them which love you, what thank *(5485)* have you?
- Luke 6:32

Charisma *(charisma, 5486)* is an obvious extension that is always a gift. The present day connotation is personal magnetic charm, appeal, or favor. This is a logical expectation since a person with tempered joy does have great appeal.

For the wages of sin is death; but the gift *(5486)* of God is eternal life through Jesus Christ our Lord.
- Romans 6:23

What are the elements of charisma? Joy is a personal, internal attitude. Grace is favor from another. Charisma is favor expressed toward another. Therefore, complete joy begins internally. In addition, we want grace from others. Furthermore, we should project charisma to others.

Calm ───────────

Peace *(eirene, 1515)* is also called prosperity. It denotes a state of untroubled, undisturbed well-being. It is the absence or end of strife. The term is sometimes rendered as rest or quietness.

An English word that is very similar to the Greek is serene. The idea is to be internally at peace and to project calm to others.

> Glory to God in the highest, and on earth peace *(1515)*, good will toward men.
> - Luke 2:14

> Daughter, be of good comfort: your faith has made you whole; go in peace *(1515)*.
> - Luke 8:48

> When a strong man, fully armed, guards his own house, his possessions are safe *(1515)*.
> - Luke 11:21 NIV

The idea is expressed succinctly in one statement. Calm replaces anxiety when our internal comfort comes from vertical influence.

> Do not be anxious about anything, but in everything, by prayer and petition, with thanksgiving, present your requests to God.
> - Philippians 4:6 NIV

HORIZONTAL
Patience ───────────

INTERNAL
+HORIZONTAL+
patience
kindness
virtue
VERTICAL

Patience *(makrothumia, 3115)* is the ability to wait without being frustrated. It is from the idea of

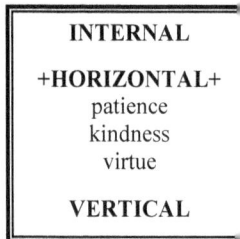

forbearance or fortitude. The waiting is from strength not from laziness. Patience is active rather than passively letting events happen.

Long suffering is a very descriptive term used in some renderings. But it is seldom heard in common usage.

> That you be not slothful, but followers of them who through faith
> and patience *(3115)* inherit the promises.
> - Hebrews 6:12

Kindness ─────────

Kindness *(crestotes, 5544)* is the one of two classes of goodness - active and passive. This is passive or benign good. That simply means there is no action associated with the idea.

It is usefulness or excellence. Other options are mellow. Various passages have used kindness, goodness, gentleness, good, easy, better, and gracious for this idea. By comparison, excellence is goodness to the highest degree.

> Behold therefore the goodness *(5544)* and severity of God: on them
> which fell, severity; but toward you, goodness, if you continue in
> his goodness: otherwise you also shall be cut off.
> - Romans 11:22

> That in the ages to come he might show the exceeding riches of his
> grace in his kindness *(5544)* toward us through Christ Jesus.
> - Ephesians 2:7

Virtue ─────────

Goodness *(agathosune, 19)* is the other of two classes of goodness - passive and active. This is the energized or active goodness. Some action is involved with the idea. This is the only word that is common to both the short and the long list of fruit. As such, it was discussed in the previous chapter.

Now know I that the LORD will do me good *(19)*...
- Judges 17:13

For so is the will of God, that with well-doing *(19)* you may put to silence the ignorance of foolish men:
- 1 Peter 2:15

VERTICAL
Confidence ─────────────

Faith *(pistis, 4102)* has taken on metaphysical components. Synonymous concepts include credence, conviction, reliance, constancy, and fidelity. Confidence is the one word that best describes the entire range of meanings.

INTERNAL
HORIZONTAL
+VERTICAL+
confidence
genteelness
control

Confidence is the mental assurance that something is true.

Since confidence or faith is a fruit of the spirit, we know it is a rational characteristic. The idea is often associated with belief. Confidence is more of an attitude based on logical arguments. Belief seems to be more emotion derived from strong desire.

Both are necessary for success. Confidence creates an atmosphere of control. In contrast, belief creates the desire to make it happen.

And he said unto them, Why are you so fearful? how is it that you have no faith *(4102)*?
- Mark 4:40

And Jesus said unto him, Go your way; your faith *(4102)* has made you healed.
- Mark 10:52

Gentlemanliness ─────────────

Gentleness *(praotes, 4236)* has been rendered many ways. Modesty and humility are two words that are often used. Some versions use meekness. Unfortunately, in current vernacular, these words carry the impression of milquetoast.

However, in no way should the term imply a wimp. The primary idea is the opposite of brashness. An excellent word that is commonly used typifies not brash.

Gentleman is the model illustration of modesty with class. Gentleman is the best way to relate this trait. The companion word for the fairer gender is lady. Both these are elements of genteel. It is easy to see how the language has related gentleness and genteelness.

> Brothers, if someone is caught in a sin, you who are spiritual should restore him gently *(4236)*.
> - Galatians 6:1 NIV

> ...to slander no one, to be peaceable and considerate, and to show true humility *(4236)* toward all men.
> - Titus 3:2 NIV

A gentleman is the epitome of distinction and is well received. A gentleman creates the desire to be like that model of a person. Someone can be a gentleman or lady at any social level. However, he is regarded as the best of his class.

A gentleman is an example of confidence, strength, nice, kind, pleasant, considerate, someone with integrity, and respect for others. In fact, gentlemanliness is the one word that best describes the entire suite of character traits. How would you describe gentleman?

Control

Temperance *(egkrateia, 1466)* is simply self-control or moderation. The word fell out of use in the earlier part of the 1900's. It was closely associated with the control of alcoholic use. Because of that unpopularity, the word has almost vanished from the language.

Control is the preferred word. Interestingly, such a strong concept is only referenced 7 times in the New Covenant.

> As Paul discoursed on righteousness, self-control *(1466)* and the
> judgment to come, Felix was afraid and said, That's enough for
> now!
> - Acts 24:25 NIV

As illustrated earlier, control is the mental function that keeps the
emotional and physical in check. Control is one of those fascinating
concepts that cross all boundaries. It is used to describe personal
actions, relationships, financial situations, and mechanical devices.
Whether in psychology, philosophy, or physics, control is crucial.

In every circumstance, control simply means to apply feedback or
constraint to a stimulus or input so that a desired response or output
is obtained. The model developed earlier demonstrates control.

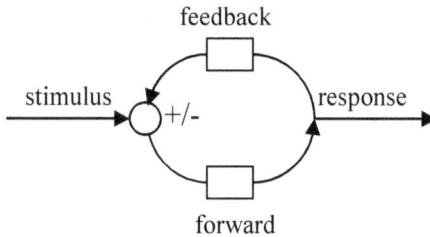

Paul, a legal expert during the first century, described the object of
control in a letter to the people at Philippi. Moderation is a related
thought.

> Let your moderation be known unto all men.
> - Philippians 4:5

Examples vary widely. A person, who is a control freak, must
dominate every situation. A ship has a rudder to control direction. A
heater has a thermostat to control temperature. Financial
expenditures are controlled to stay in a budget. In what area do you
need to have further control?

LEGAL
Legal Concepts ───────────

```
+LEGAL+
  mercy
  justice
  freedom
```

Legal concepts are not a separate category of attributes or character. These are actually parts of the other attributes and of character. Notice that the perfect attribute was the basis for all law. So a precise location for judicial characteristics would be a sub category under perfect.

Nevertheless, many authors present the ideas as independent traits. For that reason, we will discuss certain distinctions from a legal perspective.

As with any item that can be uniquely defined, there are three components. The judicial values are mercy, justice, and freedom. The alternate values we have seen are compassion, morality, and perfect relating to the law. All of these are internal or emotional facets.

Under the law, justice implies there are consequences. Mercy implies there is favorable treatment, which mitigates some of the consequences. Freedom implies making choices that concur with natural law and eliminates any consequences of concern.

Mercy ─────────────

Mercy *(eleos, 1656)* is a result of compassion applied in a legal setting. So mercy could equally be included as a component of the compassion character trait. Mercy is always a fortunate circumstance for the recipient. The English word eleemosynary, which means charity, comes from the Greek origin *(eleos, 1656)*.

Mercy is referenced 276 times throughout the manuscript. Obviously, this is an important concept.

> So then it is not of him that wills, nor of him that runs, but of God that shows mercy *(1656)*.
> - Romans 9:16

But God, who is rich in mercy *(1656)*, for his great love wherewith
he loved us...
- Ephesians 2:4

Justice ━━━━━━━━━━━

Just *(dikaios, 1342)* is translated from the exact same word as
righteous. That earlier discussion covers this concept. In terms that
are more common, morality is used for the idea. Therefore, just is
inextricably tied to morality.

> As I hear, I judge: and my judgment is just *(1342)*; because I seek
> not mine own will, but the will of the Father which has sent me.
> - John 5:30

Freedom ━━━━━━━━━━━

Free *(eleutheroo, 1659)* is perhaps one of the more emotional words
in language. Note it is derived from the same root word as mercy
(1656).

Free is almost always stated with negation of an undesirable
situation. It means unconstrained, unlimited, independent, and
uncontrolled. There is one positive word that can be used - choice.

Perfect before law, means the law has no consequences to you.
Therefore, you are free or liberated. However, freedom must be
closely guarded. When the dream or will for freedom has been
shattered, choice stops.

Being free *(nadiyb, 5081)* was as strong a desire under the Old
Covenant as it is today.

> Restore unto me the joy of your salvation; and uphold me with your
> free *(5081)* spirit.
> - Psalm 51:12

And you shall know the truth, and the truth shall make you free *(1659)*.
- John 8:32

Freedom requires personal responsibility. Any control that is transferred to another authority represents a loss of freedom.

APPLICATION
Relating an application ───────────

There is an excellent illustration of the preciseness of writings by different authors. Look at an exchange of greetings in a letter from an intellectual, Paul, to his protégé, Timothy. This is an emotional conversation, which corresponds directly to the internal fruits of the spirit - joy, compassion, and peace.

Unto Timothy, my own son in the faith: Grace, mercy, and peace...
- 1 Timothy 1:2

We have seen that the word for grace *(5489)* is derived from the word for joy *(5475)*. In addition, mercy is one of the elements of compassionate love. Then peace is obviously the calmness previously discussed. The statement could be accurately rendered with different words.

Unto Timothy, my own son in the faith: Joy, compassion, and calm...

Is it not intriguing that with understanding the few basic character traits, we can relate to anyone? Can you imagine a person with all these positive attitudes - virtue, morality, and integrity? Think about a person with all the expanded traits: compassion, charisma, and calm; patience, kindness, and virtue; confidence, gentlemanliness, and control.

What would you call that person? Do you want to be that way? These are all positive attitudes that are available. Every character trait that is associated with God is also directed toward humans. The essence of all the character traits is to be calm, in control, with class. That describes a gentleman.

Review ━━━━━━━━━━

1. How close are you to meeting the standards of character?
2. What is your greatest strength?
3. What is your weakness? It will become your strength if you develop it.
4. What is confidence?
5. What is a gentleman?

CHARACTER

Internal	Horizontal	Vertical	Relationship
emotional	physical	mental	perspective
compassion	kindness	confidence	current use
love	kindness	faith	Galatians 5
charisma	patience	gentlemanliness	current use
joy	patience	gentleness	Galatians 5
calm	virtue	control	current use
peace	goodness	temperance	Galatians 5

9

IN THE NAME OF JESUS

THOUGHT
To err is human.
To forgive is divine.

History pivot ━━━━━━━━━

The ancient record of history and religion occurred during two periods. The languages reflect the era during development. The older document was in Hebrew, the newer in Greek.

There are many parallels between the manuscripts. Both start with a pedigree or descent of a family.

The first book of the Old Record is Genesis. The name literally means the beginning. The author was Moses, a prince of Egypt trained in history and government, who became leader of the Hebrew nation.

The first book of the New Record is Matthew. Its first statement begins the genealogy, which is the lineage or family tree. The author was Matthew, a Hebrew citizen, who became a tax collector and government official in the Roman Empire.

Obviously both words, Genesis and genealogy, are derived from the same root. *Gens* is a Roman or Latin word that means a clan or related organisms.

The next parallel is in relationships. The Old Record primarily deals with the creative and emotional will of God. The New Record initially deals with the physical person of God, the man Jesus. The New Record then closes with the Spirit of a rational intellectual God. What a fascinating formula for theology - the study of God!

The first declaration of the Old Record was a simple, striking assertion of God.

> In the beginning, God...
> - Genesis 1:1

In an equally concise way, the new document gives a dramatic declaration of Jesus.

> A record of the genealogy of Jesus Christ the son of David, the son of Abraham:
> - Matthew 1:1

One record describes creation. The other record describes a birth.

The first transcript gives two identifiers for God during the creation account as well as introducing the Spirit. First, God is declared the Creator in the very first statement. Next, the Spirit of God hovered over the fluid morass in the second sentence. Finally, Yehovah God was given as his personal name during the days of creation.

The later transcript gives two identifiers for Jesus during the genealogy account. It also introduces the Spirit. First, Christ is declared the anointed in the first statement. Next, the Spirit of God hovered over Mary before the birth. Finally, Jesus was his personal name in the family tree.

What is the proper name, Jesus ───────────

Throughout most of history, names have had a meaning. A name is often derived from a location or a dramatic event.

The genealogy we are researching is for an individual named Jesus. This is a Greek version of a Hebrew name, Joshua. The connotation of his handle is described below.

> She will give birth to a son, and you are to give him the name Jesus
> *(2424)*, because he will save his people from their sins.
> - Matthew 1:21

In simplest terms, Joshua and Jesus can be stated as Jehovah *(Yehovah)* is salvation or liberator. The personal names are a direct correlation to *Yehovah*, the name of God. The proper name is representative of a man as the physical person of God.

As a further affirmation relating to the Almighty, before his birth the youngster was given another appellation. In the Greek record, he was called Immanuel *(1694)*, which is also spelled Emmanuel.

> Behold, a virgin shall be with child, and shall bring forth a son, and
> they shall call his name Immanuel *(1694)*, which being interpreted
> is, God *(2316)* with us.
> - Matthew 1:23

A transliteration from the Hebrew gives the identical name, Immanuel *(6005)*. Our earlier study included the Hebrew names of deity. We remember that *El* was an abbreviation for God *(Elohiym)*. The complete translation of Immanuel is included with the name, God with us.

The Greek translation for God is *theos (2316)*. That word is used 1343 times in the New Testament. Therefore it is safe to say that it is not restricted to an Old Testament concept.

This event was forecast about 742 years before it occurred. An ancient Hebrew prognosticator was confident enough to record the prediction.

> Behold, a virgin shall conceive, and bear a son, and shall call his
> name Immanuel *(6005)*.
> - Isaiah 7:14

Notice the similarity between the forecast and the history. The
statements are virtually identical in content. The differences are only
in the translators' arrangement of the words.

Anointed, Christ ━━━━━━━━━

Matthew's genealogy is for Jesus Christ *(5547)*, the son of David.
What is Christ? Is that a family name?

Christ is an English transliteration from a Greek adjective *christos*.
Christen has the same root. It means to name or dedicate by
ceremony.

In the Old Record, a Hebrew term was used similarly to mean
anointed or covered over with oil. The phrase was applied primarily
to the priests. They were separated, set apart, or made special by
ceremonially placing oil on parts of their anatomy, such as the ear
and toe.

Therefore, it is apparent that the adjective Christ is related to
worship and deity. Christ is related to the emotional will of God.

The equivalent word is Messiah from the Hebrew *Mashiyach
(4822)*. That word was translated anointed on 37 occasions and
Messiah on only two. In current usage, the word means liberator

> Know therefore and understand, that from the going forth of the
> commandment to restore and to build Jerusalem unto the Messiah
> *(4822)* the Prince shall be seven weeks, and sixty-two weeks: the
> street shall be built again, and the wall, even in troublous times.
>
> And after sixty- two weeks shall Messiah *(4822)* be cut off, but not
> for himself:
> - Daniel 9:25-26

Only Daniel, a scion of a royal Hebrew family, who wrote in
Aramaic has the word transliterated as Messiah. Daniel had
tremendous integrity and focus on the Almighty. From his
communications with the Most High, Daniel had the ability to

interpret dreams and visions. This unique person rose to tremendous political power.

The Babylonian king, Nebuchadnezzar, overthrew the government of Daniel's country. Nevertheless, Daniel became Prime Minister under Nebuchadnezzar. He continued in the post under Belshazzar, a son of Nebuchadnezzar. That kingdom was consolidated under the rule of the Medes and the Persians. Daniel continued to prosper under Darius, the son of Ahasuerus, the Median king over Chaldea. He even maintained the position under Cyrus, king of Persia.

Can you imagine what kind of person Daniel must have been? He was taken into captivity as a young man. Then he became a Prime Minister under at least four foreign governments. His record keeping and writing undoubtedly was impeccable.

A hovering, Spirit ━━━━━━━━━━

The birth of the child Jesus was extraordinary in every sense of the word. To establish the inimitable relationship, an extended portion of Matthew's report in the New Record is registered.

This is how the birth of Jesus Christ came about: His mother Mary was pledged to be married to Joseph, but before they came together, she was found to be with child through the Holy Spirit.

Because Joseph her husband was a righteous man and did not want to expose her to public disgrace, he had in mind to divorce her quietly.

But after he had considered this, an angel of the Lord appeared to him in a dream and said, Joseph son of David, do not be afraid to take Mary home as your wife, because what is conceived in her is from the Holy Spirit.

She will give birth to a son, and you are to give him the name Jesus, because he will save his people from their sins.

All this took place to fulfill what the Lord had said through the prophet:

The virgin will be with child and will give birth to a son, and they will call him Immanuel which means, God with us.
- Matthew 1:18-23 NIV

Who were the mother and father of Jesus? His ancestors are considered in a later chapter. Here we will only deal with his parents.

As stated in the prediction by Isaiah, the mother would be a virgin. In combination with specific declarations by the tax collector, Matthew, virgin asserts no sexual contact. Mary had not come together with her fiancé Joseph. Then how was the child fathered?

The name Immanuel explains that the Father was God. The public official further enlightens that the particular member involved with conception was the Spirit.

Jesus declared he was the Son of Man on multiple occasions. In one instance, he said that he and the Father were the same. That is in complete concert with the realization that God and every being in his image is a trinity.

I and my Father *(3962)* are one.
- John 10:30

The Greek derivative for father is *pater (3962)*. Of the 419 times it is used in the New Testament, it refers to Deity procreator 268 times.

The person Jesus had a physical, human mother. His father was God through the work of the Spirit. In ancient mythology, this combination was called a demigod. Jesus was completely God through the lineage of his father. He was completely man through the lineage of his mother.

It should be noted that Jesus did not call himself the Son of God. Jesus referred to The Father on several occasions. It should be observed in the tradition of the time that the name of God could not be spoken, but was used euphemistically. The choice of calling God as The Father was totally in keeping with the commands of the religious leaders.

This unique relationship has only been documented one time throughout the history of mankind. Because of this special bond, Jesus has had more impact on the human race than any other person.

A title, Lord ──────────

In addition to a proper name and an adjective of worship, Jesus took on a title. He was frequently called Lord. Since he did not object to the label, it is obvious that he accepted and approved it.

Jesus' cousin John first applied the designation. John was the son of Elizabeth, who was a cousin of Mary, the mother of Jesus.

> And behold, your cousin Elizabeth...
> - Luke 1:36

John was an itinerate evangelist. Because of his message, he was called the Baptizer or Baptist. He was an orator in the countryside that challenged people to repent and turn to God. His attire was animal skin and he ate honey and wildlife from the land. When Jesus was ready to go public, John proclaimed the message.

> A voice of one calling in the desert, Prepare the way for the Lord (2962), make straight paths for him.
> - Matthew 3:3 NIV

Lord is from the Greek kurios (2962). It is used 748 times and was translated lord, master, or sir.

A full house ──────────

Jesus is the proper name given to the young boy by his parents. Lord is the title bestowed because of his role as a teacher. Christ describes the office or job he holds as the anointed Messiah or liberator. The appropriate combination is Lord Jesus, the Christ. In many cases the comma is dropped so the office appears as part of the name.

A corresponding example can be found in many illustrations in current life. My name given by my parents is Marcus Durham. In our culture, we use two or more names. The second is the family name. My title is Doctor because of my education. My office or job is Professor at the University. Another office is President of our companies. Hence, the combination is Doctor Marcus Durham, Professor, or Doctor Marcus Durham, President.

There is no implication that I am at the level of the Lord Jesus. This is simply an illustration of the relationship between the different terms.

After John proclaimed who Jesus was, John baptized him. When he was coming from the water, the complete trinity was revealed simultaneously.

> And Jesus, when he was baptized, went up straightway out of the water: and, lo, the heavens were opened unto him, and he saw the Spirit of God descending like a dove, and lighting upon him: And lo a voice from heaven, saying, This is my beloved Son, in whom I am well pleased.
> - Matthew 3:16

The man Jesus was physically on the earth. The spirit was in the air and floated like a dove. The Creator, God the Father, spoke from heaven with emotion. This is a very limited circumstance where the trinity of God is apparent at the same time.

Although not apparent to the five senses, all three members are mentioned together as Jesus was leaving the planet in Matthew 28. There is another recorded instance where the three are observed simultaneously. A corresponding encounter is reported at the end of time in Revelation 22.

I Am ──────────

After leaving John, Jesus' spirit led him into the remote regions of the country. There he faced all possible temptations, tests, and trials. Because of his unique position, the ultimate adversary personally challenged him.

He was tried on three different fronts. He was challenged mentally and responded with an intellectual argument speaking words. Word in this case is from the Greek *rhema (4487)*, which is a spoken word or sentence. The Greek *logos (3056)* is also translated word but it means study or knowledge.

> It is written, Man shall not live by bread alone, but by every word *(rhema, 4487)* that proceeds out of the mouth of God.
> - Mathew 4:4

He was challenged with physical health and responded with a direct command about teasing.

> It is written again, You shall not tempt the Lord your God.
> - Mathew 4:7

He was challenged emotionally with power and responded that he already had everything you could want. Worship, as we have seen earlier, is related to the adjective Christ.

> Get you hence, Satan: for it is written, You shall worship *(proskuneo, 4352)* the Lord your God, and him only shall you serve.
> - Mathew 4:10

Jesus himself made the most direct affirmation of his regal position. He asserted he was proclaiming the precepts of the Lord and God. This point was immediately prior to the public being aware of him. He had been a carpenter and was now prepared to be the conscience of people, a nation, and the world.

Your commission ━━━━━━━━━━━━

At the conclusion of his time on this planet, Jesus reaffirmed his power. He declared the trinity relationship as his final act. The verses are added in some texts and not included in others.

> All power is given unto me in heaven and in earth.
>
> Go you therefore, and teach all nations, baptizing them in the name of the Father, and of the Son, and of the Holy Ghost:
>
> Teaching them to observe all things whatsoever I have commanded you: and, lo, I am with you always, even unto the end of the world. Amen.
> - Matthew 28:18-20

This picture of baptism mirrors the event in Jesus' immersion. The three members of God are succinctly stated. The Father is the Creator God. The Son is the physical person Yehovah on the earth. The Spirit is in the air that continues to dominate during the present time.

In addition, Jesus established his power as the one complete God. He transferred the full authority to those who follow his teaching. Do you live as if you have that authority? Do you teach others they can have the power to do all things through Yehovah?

> I can do all things through Christ who strengthens me.
> - Philippians 4:13

A composite picture ━━━━━━━━━━━

The man Jesus had tremendous impact on the world or culture of his day. Because of his creative nature, he had impact on the founding of the world or planet. In his comforting position, he continues to influence the most powerful thoughts of the world and people today.

It was not until he had left the earth that anyone realized really who he was. He led a cadre of twelve interns, called apostles, who personally studied with him for three years.

> Now the names of the twelve apostles are these; The first, Simon, who is called Peter, and Andrew his brother; James the son of Zebedee, and John his brother; Philip, and Bartholomew; Thomas, and Matthew the tax-collector; James the son of Alphaeus, and Lebbaeus, whose surname was Thaddaeus; Simon the Canaanite, and Judas Iscariot, who also betrayed him.
> - Matthew 10:2

The first listed is Peter. He was the most visible of the group, and appeared to be the spokesman. With the exit of Jesus, all but one of these eventually continued in the work established by him. It was some weeks later that Peter, the fisherman, businessman, and theologian, put it all together. He gave the first account of the complete recognition of who Jesus was.

> So if God gave them the same gift as he gave us, who believed in the Lord Jesus Christ, who was I to think that I could oppose God?
> - Acts 11:17 NIV

From this point forward, the apostles and the writers of inspired letters used the label Lord Jesus Christ. For the two thousand years of history since that time, the brand has continued to be revered. That name is a summation of everything you can know about *Who Is This God?*

The final curtain ━━━━━━━━━

The last book of the anthology of Christian religion is called the Revelation or the Apocalypse. The name implies there are things to be uncovered, unveiled, or revealed. The first comment in the book begins with the anointed man Jesus. It affirms that God has communicated with him. Then it avers that the information is for those who serve with Jesus.

> The Revelation of Jesus Christ, which God gave unto him, to show
> unto his servants...
> - Revelation 1:1

What a powerful observation. It goes on to proclaim a blessing,
favor, or prosperity. The encouragement is to those that read or hear
the words and do the things written in it.

The final chapter comes to a close. In the final scenes, it reveals the
trinity relationship of God. The three components of the name of
Jesus are also noted. In verse 16, Jesus is talking. In verse 17, the
Spirit is influencing. In verse 18, God is emotionally warning. The
very last line of the play gives the title, the name, and the adjective
for the man Jesus. He is God in a physical body. As a final act,
favor is given to mankind.

> The grace of our Lord Jesus Christ be with you all. Amen.
> - Revelation 22:21

The record has shown that the names associated with Jesus are
special. One other passage summarizes the power that is associated
with it. There is a special beauty of this affirmation.

> If you shall ask anything in my name, I will do it.
> - John 14:14

The total power of God is transferred to you, if you will claim the
name of Jesus. Are there any exceptions in the affirmation? Is this
only religious or does it apply to everyday life? Do you believe the
manuscript is accurate on all accounts? Do you live by the authority
that is invested in you?

The purpose of the study of the names is so you can have complete
authority in all aspects of your life. This power comes by
understanding this history and philosophy and how it is available to
you.

Review ——————————

Complete each question.

1. What is the proper name of the God-man?
2. What adjective relates to worship?
3. What title was first given by John?
4. What three names combined are commonly used to identify the physical person of God?
5. What is the relationship of God to Mary's youngster?
6. The dove was which member of God?
7. What is the primary command, stated twice in the Commission?
8. How can we get anything done?

NAMES

Emotional	Physical	Intellectual	Relationship
God	Jesus	Spirit	members
Father	Son	Holy Spirit	familial

Office	Name	Title	Explanation
Christ	Jesus	Lord	address
Christos	Jesus	kurios	Greek
annointed	given name	sir	equivalent

10

TITLES, TAGS, & TERMS

Thought
People do business with people they like.
MOD

What's up ━━━━━━━━━━━━━

Jesus is the given name of the most well-known person in history. He was a successful teacher, reputable religious leader, a popular coach and mentor, as well as physical representation of Deity. As a result, he was called by many titles, tags, and terms.

An earlier chapter of our work gave his particular names. This chapter will observe other appendages to those names. The list is myriad. There are over 250 events and instances recorded about the life of the most remarkable man. To keep the task manageable, we will only refer to some 75 of those.

Our references will primarily be those recorded by the notable government official, Matthew. The list encompasses the entire chronicle of Matthew with a few excerpts from other authors. Therefore, it is an excellent summary of the life of a super man.

Just as his birth was unique, so was his departing this physical planet. There has been only one virgin birth. Likewise, there has been only one who has returned three days after his demise, by his own power.

Forecast ────────────

Perhaps one of the most familiar groupings of names was a prediction of things to come. Isaiah, an ancient seer, wrote this declaration about 742 years before the event.

> For unto us a child is born, unto us a son is given: and the government shall be upon his shoulder: and his name shall be called wonderful Counsellor, the mighty God, the everlasting Father, the Prince of Peace.
> - Isaiah 9:6

Son of Abraham ────────────

> A record of the genealogy of Jesus Christ the son of David, the son of Abraham:
> - Matthew 1:1 NIV

Birth ────────────

> This is how the birth of Jesus Christ came about:
> - Matthew 1:18 NIV

Son of Mary ────────────

> This is how the birth of Jesus Christ came about: His mother Mary...
> - Matthew 1:18 NIV

Son of virgin ────────────

> The virgin will be with child and will give birth to a son...
> - Matthew 1:23 NIV

God with us

...and they will call him Immanuel which means, God with us.
- Matthew 1:23 NIV

From Bethlehem

After Jesus was born in Bethlehem in Judea...
- Matthew 2:1 NIV

King of Jews

Where is the one who has been born king of the Jews? We saw his star in the east and have come to worship him.
- Matthew 2:2 NIV

Governor

...for out of you shall come a Governor, that shall rule my people Israel.
- Matthew 2:6

Young child

And when they were come into the house, they saw the young child with Mary his mother...
- Matthew 2:11

Worshipped as royalty

...and fell down, and worshipped him: and when they had opened their treasures, they presented unto him gifts; gold, and frankincense, and myrrh.
- Matthew 2:11

From Egypt ────────────

When he arose, he took the young child and his mother by night,
and departed into Egypt: ... Out of Egypt have I called my son.
- Matthew 2:14-15

From Nazareth ────────────

And he came and dwelt in a city called Nazareth: that it might be
fulfilled which was spoken by the prophets, He shall be called a
Nazarene.
- Matthew 2:23

Lamb of God ────────────

The next day John saw Jesus coming toward him and said, Look,
the Lamb of God, who takes away the sin of the world!
- John 1:29 NIV

Lord ────────────

Prepare ye the way of the Lord, make his paths straight.
- Matthew 3:3

Worthy ────────────

...whose shoes I am not worthy to bear: he shall baptize you with
the Holy Ghost, and with fire:
- Matthew 3:11

From Galilee ────────────

Then came Jesus from Galilee to Jordan unto John, to be baptized
of him.
- Matthew 3:13

Beloved Son ━━━━━━━━━

…And lo a voice from heaven, saying, This is my beloved Son, in whom I am well pleased.
- Matthew 3:17 NIV

Tempted ━━━━━━━━━

Then was Jesus led up of the Spirit into the wilderness to be tempted of the devil.
- Matthew 4:1

Hungry ━━━━━━━━━

And when he had fasted forty days and forty nights, he was afterward hungry.
- Matthew 4:2

The word spoken━━━━━━━━━

Jesus answered, It is written: Man does not live on bread alone, but on every word (*rheema, 4487*) that comes from the mouth of God.
- Matthew 4:4 NIV

The word of knowledge ━━━━━━━━━

In the beginning was the Word (*logos, 3056*), and the Word was with God, and the Word was God.
- John 1:1

Angel protectors ━━━━━━━━━

He will command his angels concerning you, and they will lift you up in their hands, so that you will not strike your foot against a stone.

- Matthew 4:6 NIV

Ahead of Satan ━━━━━━━━━━

Then said Jesus unto him, Get you hence, Satan: for it is written, you shall worship the Lord your God, and him only shall you serve.
- Matthew 4:10

From Capernaum ━━━━━━━━━━

Leaving Nazareth, he went and lived in Capernaum, which was by the lake in the area of Zebulun and Naphtali...
- Matthew 4:13 NIV

Preacher ━━━━━━━━━

From that time on Jesus began to preach, Repent, for the kingdom of heaven is near.
- Matthew 4:17 NIV

Walker ━━━━━━━━━

As Jesus was walking beside the Sea of Galilee...
- Matthew 4:18 NIV

Leader ━━━━━━━━

Come, follow me, Jesus said...
- Matthew 4:19 NIV

Fishers of men ━━━━━━━━━

Come, follow me, Jesus said, and I will make you fishers of men.
- Matthew 4:19 NIV

Water to wine ━━━━━━━━━━━━

...and the master of the banquet tasted the water that had been turned into wine. He did not realize where it had come from, though the servants who had drawn the water knew.
- John 2:9 NIV

Miraculous signs ━━━━━━━━━━━

This, the first of his miraculous signs, Jesus performed at Cana in Galilee.
- John 2:11 NIV

Mountaineer ━━━━━━━━━━━━

And seeing the multitudes, he went up into a mountain: and when he was set, his disciples came unto him:
- Matthew 5:1 NIV

Blessed people ━━━━━━━━━━━

...and he began to teach them, saying: Blessed...
- Matthew 5:3 NIV

Lawyer ━━━━━━━━━━

Do not think that I have come to abolish the Law or the Prophets; I have not come to abolish them but to fulfill them.
- Matthew 5:17 NIV

Applications ━━━━━━━━━━━

You have heard that it was said... But I tell you that...
- Matthew 5:21 NIV

Rewarder ━━━━━━━━━━

Be careful not to do your acts of righteousness before men, to be seen by them. If you do, you will have no reward from your Father in heaven.
- Matthew 6:1 NIV

One who prays ━━━━━━━━━━━━

This, then, is how you should pray:

Our Father in heaven, hallowed be your name, your kingdom come, your will be done on earth as it is in heaven. Give us today our daily bread. Forgive us our debts, as we also have forgiven our debtors. And lead us not into temptation, but deliver us from the evil one. Amen.
- Matthew 6:9 NIV

Fasted ━━━━━━━━━━

When you fast, do not look somber as the hypocrites do, for they disfigure their faces to show men they are fasting.
- Matthew 6:16 NIV

Light ━━━━━━━━━━

If then the light within you is darkness, how great is that darkness!
- Matthew 6:23 NIV

In him was life, and that life was the light of men. The light shines in the darkness, but the darkness has not understood it.
- John 1:4-5 NIV

Life ━━━━━━━━━━

In him was life, and that life was the light of men.
- John 1:4 NIV

Seeker ━━━━━━━━

...But seek first his kingdom and his righteousness, and all these
things will be given to you as well.
- Matthew 6:33 NIV

Amazing ━━━━━━━━

When Jesus had finished saying these things, the crowds were
amazed at his teaching...
- Matthew 7:28 NIV

Large crowds ━━━━━━━━

When he came down from the mountainside, large crowds followed
him.
- Matthew 8:1 NIV

Not susceptible to disease ━━━━━━━━

A man with leprosy came and knelt before him and said, Lord, if
you are willing, you can make me clean. Jesus reached out his hand
and touched the man.
- Matthew 8:3 NIV

Healer ━━━━━━━━

And when Jesus was come in Peter's house, he saw his wife's
mother lying and sick of a fever. And he touched her hand and the
fever left her;
- Matthew 8:15

Substitute ━━━━━━━━

That it might be fulfilled which was spoken by Isaiah, the prophet,
saying, He himself took our infirmities, and bore our sicknesses.

- Matthew 8:17

Teacher ━━━━━━━━━

Then a teacher of the law came to him and said, Teacher, I will
follow you wherever you go.
- Matthew 8:19 NIV

What kind of man ━━━━━━━━━

The men were amazed and asked, what kind of man is this? Even
the winds and the waves obey him!
- Matthew 8:27 NIV

Demon dominator ━━━━━━━━━

The demons begged Jesus, If you drive us out, send us into the herd
of pigs.
- Matthew 8:31 NIV

Sailor ━━━━━━━━━

Jesus stepped into a boat, crossed over and came to his own town.
- Matthew 9:1 NIV

Forgive sins ━━━━━━━━━

Take heart, son; your sins are forgiven.
- Matthew 9:2 NIV

Son of Man ━━━━━━━━━

…But so that you may know that the Son of Man has authority on
earth to forgive sins.

- Matthew 9:6 NIV

Son of David ━━━━━━━━━

As Jesus went on from there, two blind men followed him; calling out, Have mercy on us, Son of David!
- Matthew 9:27 NIV

Lord of Sabbath ━━━━━━━━━

...For the Son of Man is Lord of the Sabbath.
- Matthew 12:8 NIV

Natural family ━━━━━━━━━

He replied to him, Who is my mother, and who are my brothers?
- Matthew 12:48 NIV

Isn't his mother's name Mary, and aren't his brothers James, Joseph, Simon and Judas?
- Matthew 13:55 NIV

Adopted family ━━━━━━━━━

Pointing to his disciples, he said, Here are my mother and my brothers. For whoever does the will of my Father in heaven is my brother and sister and mother.
- Matthew 12:49-50 NIV

Carpenter ━━━━━━━━━

Isn't this the carpenter's son?
- Matthew 13:55 NIV

Prophet ━━━━━━━━

But Jesus said to them, Only in his hometown and in his own house
is a prophet without honor.
- Matthew 13:57 NIV

Not respected by family ━━━━━━━

But Jesus said to them, Only in his hometown and in his own house
is a prophet without honor.
- Matthew 13:57 NIV

Ghost ━━━━━━

When the disciples saw him walking on the lake, they were
terrified. It's a ghost, they said, and cried out in fear.
- Matthew 14:26 NIV

Who do people say ━━━━━━

When Jesus came to the region of Caesarea Philippi, he asked his
disciples, Who do people say the Son of Man is?
- Matthew 16:13 NIV

Who do you say ━━━━━━

But what about you? he asked. Who do you say I am? Simon Peter
answered, You are the Christ, the Son of the living God.
- Matthew 16:15-16 NIV

Door ━━━━━━

I am the door: by me if any man enter in, he shall be saved, and
shall go in and out, and find pasture.
- John 10:9

Good Shepherd ——————

I am the good shepherd: the good shepherd gives his life for the sheep
- John 10:11

Way, truth, and life ——————

Jesus said unto him, I am the way, the truth, and the life: no man comes unto the Father, but by me.
- John 14:6

Vine ——————

I am the true vine, and my Father is the gardener.
- John 15:1 NIV

From Nazareth ——————

The crowds answered, This is Jesus, the prophet from Nazareth in Galilee.
- Matthew 21:11 NIV

Capstone ——————

Jesus said to them, Have you never read in the Scriptures: The stone the builders rejected has become the capstone; the Lord has done this, and it is marvelous in our eyes?
- Matthew 21:42 NIV

Man of integrity ——————

…they said, we know you are a man of integrity and that you teach the way of God in accordance with the truth.
- Matthew 22:16 NIV

Name of Lord ━━━━━━━━

For I tell you, you will not see me again until you say, Blessed is he who comes in the name of the Lord.
- Matthew 23:39 NIV

Rabbi ━━━━━━━━

Then Judas, the one who would betray him, said, Surely not I, Rabbi?
- Matthew 26:25 NIV

King of Jews ━━━━━━━━

Meanwhile Jesus stood before the governor, and the governor asked him, Are you the king of the Jews?
- Matthew 27:11 NIV

Innocent man ━━━━━━━━

While Pilate was sitting on the judge's seat, his wife sent him this message, Don't have anything to do with that innocent man, for I have suffered a great deal today in a dream because of him.
- Matthew 27:19 NIV

King of Israel ━━━━━━━━

He's the King of Israel! Let him come down now from the cross, and we will believe in him.
- Matthew 27:42 NIV

Crucified

The angel said to the women, do not be afraid, for I know that you are looking for Jesus, who was crucified.
- Matthew 28:5 NIV

Risen

He is not here; he has risen, just as he said. Come and see the place where he lay.
- Matthew 28:6 NIV

Comforter

Then Jesus said to them, do not be afraid. Go and tell my brothers to go to Galilee; there they will see me.
- Matthew 28:10 NIV

Vulnerable

Then he said to Thomas, Put your finger here; see my hands. Reach out your hand and put it into my side. Stop doubting and believe.
- John 20:27 NIV

Aviator

While he was blessing them, he left them and was taken up into heaven.
- Luke 24:51 NIV

Review

Everything in the Teachings was given as an illustration or guide, whether history or theology. It is for the personal use of individuals and not reserved for arcane religious use.

1. Discuss what each of the descriptions mean and how it relates to you.
2. As a broadening experience, see how many other descriptors and names you can find?

11

GENEALOGY 101 - PRE-DELUGE

Thought
You may be looking.
Are you seeing?

History pivot ━━━━━━━━━━━━

The entire account of the ancient manuscript is about *Who Is This God?* The Hebrew Scripture is a history about the family of one man, Jesus the Messiah or Liberator. The New Document begins with his genealogy. Therefore, the complete manuscript was simply foretelling, telling, or retelling his story.

There are numerous family trees recorded throughout the volume. The major lineages are identified below.

Genesis 5 relates the generations of Adam up to Noah. Genesis 10 records the sons of Noah up to the separation of Pangea, the global continent. Genesis 11 reflects the generations of Shem up to Abraham.

Exodus 1:1 is an accounting of the names of the children of Israel or Jacob. Exodus 6:14 yields the family record of Moses and Aaron. This was not part of the royal messianic line. Ruth 4:18 has a brief pedigree from Pharez to Boaz and Ruth then on to David.

I Chronicles 1 - 3 was recorded after the return from Babylon. It provides a recapitulation from Adam to the sons of Zerubbabel.

Matthew 1 is the family tree from Abraham forward to Jesus. Luke 3:28 gives the forebears from Jesus backwards to Adam.

COMMON LINE
Adam
Seth
Enos
Cainan
Mahalaleel
Jared
Enoch
Methuselah
Lamech
Noah

The fact that very explicit family trees are listed not once but twice indicates the importance of their study. These obviously were intended to relate the man, Jesus, to the entire history of the Old Testament. Therefore, to fully understand *Who Is This God?* it is incumbent to understand the background and history.

To that end, we will look at an overview of the significant historical characters and events. This will necessarily involve many situations that preceded the natural birth of the God-man, Jesus. The entire history of the Hebrew Old Testament points to this event.

Messianic prophecy and promise ────────────

Ten distinct instances in the Old Canon are related as messianic prophecies. These are identifications about the seed of individuals. Seed is an old euphemism for offspring or progeny. In each case, the promise is that a descendent will overcome some circumstance. These are all culminated in the birth of the Messiah.

The first promise starts at the Garden of Eden. Six of the prophecies are in the book of beginnings, Genesis. The seventh is the crowning event; it is the promise for the son of David, the King. Two forecasts have to do with prophecy of the birth. Then the ultimate prediction was for the final regent of the universe.

At the Garden of Eden, the relationship between humans and the enemy serpent was defined. The offspring of the woman was to eventually be the Messiah or liberator of the nation and humankind.

And I will put enmity between you and the woman, and between
your offspring and hers; he will crush your head, and you will strike
his heel.
- Genesis 3:15 NIV

The family tree was branched through Shem, a son of Noah.

And he said, Blessed be the LORD God of Shem; and Canaan shall
be his servant.
- Genesis 9:26

Abraham became the father of many nations and the father of faith.

...and through your offspring all nations on earth will be blessed,
because you have obeyed me.
- Genesis 22:18 NIV

The line was refined at Isaac, his son.

I will make your descendants as numerous as the stars in the sky
and will give them all these lands, and through your offspring all
nations on earth will be blessed...
- Genesis 26:4 NIV

The family tree narrowed again with Jacob, called Israel.

Your descendants will be like the dust of the earth, and you will
spread out to the west and to the east, to the north and to the south.
All peoples on earth will be blessed through you and your offspring.
- Genesis 28:14 NIV

The tribe of Judah would be the selected line for the kingship.

The sceptre shall not depart from Judah, nor a lawgiver from
between his feet, until Shiloh come; and unto him shall the
gathering of the people be.
- Genesis 49:10

The seventh prophecy is narrowed to the son of David, the King.

When your days are over and you rest with your fathers, I will raise up your offspring to succeed you, who will come from your own body, and I will establish his kingdom.
- II Samuel 7:12

The birth was to a virgin maid.

Therefore the Lord himself shall give you a sign; Behold, a virgin shall conceive, and bear a son, and shall call his name Immanuel.
- Isaiah 7:14

The location of the birth would be the small, non-descript community of Bethlehem.

But you, Bethlehem Ephratah, though you are little among the thousands of Judah, yet out of you shall he come forth unto me that is to be ruler in Israel; whose goings forth have been from of old, from everlasting.
- Micah 5:2

The future regent of the universe was described in his regal appellations.

For unto us a child is born, unto us a son is given: and the government shall be upon his shoulder: and his name shall be called wonderful Counselor, the mighty God, the everlasting Father, the Prince of Peace.
- Isaiah 9:6

History repeats itself ─────────────

The promises are an overview of the lineage of the Messiah. Our research will now focus on more of the background and the impact on the human race.

The phrase 'these are the generations of' is repeated more than 10 times in Genesis alone. It is duplicated many more times in other parts of the Hebrew and the Greek anthology. However, the phrase 'book of the generation' is applied to only two of the reports.

The first account is the book of Adam in Genesis 5. This is the record of the first mortal man with his fallibility. The second account is the book of Jesus Christ in Matthew 1. It is the record of immortal man and his perfection.

Because there is so much of human tradition to cover, it will be broken into three chapters. This chapter is primarily involved with establishing the common lineage of all mankind up to the deluge. The next chapter will address the human family up to the separation into language groups. The succeeding chapter will address the Semitic language group with focus on the king line.

The initial heritage is documented in Genesis 5. The book is a record of the history following Adam. It is not a detailed account of his origins. Nevertheless, there is a nugget overview of the genesis of Adam.

God created man in the likeness of God. Male and female were created. God blessed them and called his name Adam. This is from the Hebrew word for mankind or ruddy *(adam, 120)*. Adam was the very first recorded human.

What about ages ━━━━━━━━━

The ages given in the traditional translation have been critically analyzed. Critics often treat the extended times as myth or legend. However, other archaeological records give exceedingly long life to kings during the same era. The Weld-Blundell Prism contains a very detailed list of monarchs including eight antediluvian kings who reigned over lower Sumeria.

These Mesopotamian kings had a rule very similar to the period of the Noah timing. The lifetime of the Genesis patriarchs seems very compatible with contemporary extra-biblical records. There appears to be a correspondence between these Sumerian rulers and the patriarchs that preceded the deluge. The average lifetime is even shorter after the flood, just as in the Genesis account.

Regardless of the timing, it is apparent that people lived for a very extended time before the deluge. One theory is called the "Canopy" or "Greenhouse" effect. This proposes that the earth was covered with a water vapor canopy.

The vapor shielded the earth from ultraviolet rays and other space phenomenon. The canopy provided a climatic controlled environment, which aided phenomenal growth. The shell burst to provide part of the floodwaters. After the flood, the lifetime began to decay until a steady state value of 70 years was reached during the time of David.

Ussher in time ———————

A second criticism challenges using the sum of the ages to arrive at elapsed time. Ussher, an early theologian, used this method to establish Adam near an estimated 4004 BC. The primary argument pitched against this dating is the use of the word begat. Some argue the word can be used for an immediate offspring as well as for grandchildren. This seems to be a tedious argument.

I Chronicles 1 gives a similar list to that given in Genesis. There are a few name differences. However, they are not sufficient to disregard the sequence in both accounts.

The discussion must also consider the Matthew 1 account. The pattern of 14 generations between major events is well established in verse 17.

> So all the generations from Abraham to David are fourteen generations; and from David until the carrying away into Babylon are fourteen generations; and from the carrying away into Babylon unto Christ are fourteen generations.
> - Matthew 1:17

No practices should be built on these calculations. Nevertheless, the pattern is intriguing enough to lend credence to the completeness of the genealogy.

All manner of arguments can be proposed about the authenticity and accuracy of the numbering system. Regardless of the contention, certain standing is achieved simply by having this detailed list. In addition, the record has persisted in common use for 3500 years of human history. No other document has that credibility.

Cautionary dating ━━━━━━━━━━

Jewish tradition places Anno Mundi at 3761 BC. A date of about 5500 BC is based on the Septuagint with the dates about 4000 BC based on the Masoretic texts.

All the dates are built on traditions, with some of the times appearing to be representational rather than actual. The entire discussion is about perspective and relational events, and should not be considered as affirmative or dogmatic.

The spitting image ━━━━━━━━━━

What do people look like? Seth looked like his dad. That is not surprising.

> And Adam...begat a son in his own likeness, after his image;
> - Genesis 5:3

But consider the declaration about his dad in the sentence just prior to this observation. The same comment is made. Adam looked like God. Period. What does God look like? People!

> ...God created man, in the likeness of God created he him.
> - Genesis 5:1

This is radical theology to some. Arguments that are more esoteric have God as some ethereal creature. That rendition is used since God is superior to all created beings. There is no argument about that fact. Nevertheless, the record is clear that people look just like God.

A theophany is a representation of God in human form. There are several records of an encounter with a theophany throughout the Old Testament. Every account clearly illustrates the human likeness.

For whom the bell tolls

Adam lived and he died. Adam's third son, Seth, was born when he was 130. That was just the beginning. He fathered more sons and daughters. His final age was 930 years. That is nearly 1000 years.

However, his venture in the garden finally caught up with him. Death was promised if he ate the forbidden fruit. He had the potential for immortality. But he chose instant gratification and mind-expanding experiences.

The fallibility of his body was passed to his progeny. The finality of the experience is shown for the remaining characters in the play of life. Each was born, gave birth to children, lived a long life, and died.

As we investigate the history, not all descendants are discussed. Only those that are significant to the line of the Messiah are maintained. This is, in reality, the book of the forefathers of Jesus Christ.

A notable exception

There are three notable exceptions to the life cycle, Enoch, Elijah, and Moses. Enoch walked with God. Enoch was the seventh generation from the creation in the line of Seth. This corresponded with Lamech I, the son of Methushael in the family of Cain, one of Adam's other sons.

> And Enoch walked with God: and he was not; for God took him.
> - Genesis 5:24

What a contrast between Enoch and Lamech I. Lamech I was patently evil. According to his own account, he deserved a greater magnitude of punishment than what Cain received.

Enoch lived a normal, mortal life just like others. He was born, fathered children, and lived for a total of 365 years. However, he was different. He walked with God.

He did not die but simply walked into the next life. This only happened explicitly to one other person, Elijah. Compare the record in the chronicles of the kings.

> And it came to pass, as they still went on, and talked, that, behold, there appeared a chariot of fire, and horses of fire, and parted them both asunder; and Elijah went up by a whirlwind into heaven.
> - II Kings 2:11

The account is less clear about Moses. He may have simply walked on across, since he was seen at the Mount of Transfiguration. Contrast Deuteronomy 34:6 with Matthew 17:3.

> So Moses the servant of the LORD died there in the land of Moab, according to the word of the LORD. And he buried him in a valley in the land of Moab, over against Bethpeor: but no man knows of his sepulchre unto this day.
> - Deuteronomy 34:5-6

> Just then there appeared before them Moses and Elijah, talking with Jesus.
> - Matthew 17:3 NIV

For those interested in numerics, Enoch provides an interesting break. He was the seventh patriarch in the family line. The number seven is associated with completeness or perfection. Then Enoch would represent perfect of mankind. This is fascinating considering his ancestry. The numerics also indicate his life was a watershed event.

The Hall of Fame in the ancient chronicles is described in Hebrews 11. This record gives a more detailed account of the character of Enoch.

> By faith Enoch was translated that he should not see death; and was not found, because God had translated him: for before his translation he had this testimony, that he pleased God.
> - Hebrews 11:5

He was translated, which means he did not see death. Before his translation, he had this reputation: he pleased God. How did he please God? By his faith!

Can anyone else have this credit? Perhaps, but it would not be in the same way. Nevertheless, we can definitely have a pleasing relationship according to the next stanza.

> Without faith, it is impossible to please him: for he that comes to God must believe that he is, and he is a rewarder of them that diligently seek him.
> - Hebrews 11:6

Ancient of ancients

Methuselah was the son of Enoch. All the days of Methuselah were 969 years. His dad was not around as long as some other parents. In contrast, according to the record, Methuselah lived to be older than any other person. Nevertheless, he too died the way of Adam.

His name literally means when he is dead, it shall be sent. This is a promise of God that he would hold off the flood and judgment as long as Methuselah lived. He outlived his father and his son. He lived 782 years after his son Lamech II was born.

All the days of Lamech II were 777. Lamech II was a son of Methuselah and the father of Noah. Obviously, he was in the surviving, more moral line of people before the deluge. Is there a reason that Lamech II lived the unusual span of years that he did?

First, the number of years is interesting. He lived for three sevens or 777 years. If seven represents perfection, and three represents the trinity, then Lamech II's years are phenomenal. The end of his life is the culmination of a dispensation of God's relationship with mortals.

Preparation for a new beginning ——————

We find that Lamech II lived 595 years after his son Noah was born. Methuselah lived 5 years longer than his son Lamech II. Genesis 7:6 states Noah was 600 years old when the flood came. Therefore, Methuselah died immediately before the flood. Tradition tells that it started raining on the day he died. His name was most appropriate.

The human race began with Adam. After the Garden episode, there was another beginning with different insights in a different world. Noah had constructed a vessel before the deluge. The boat was to carry the third beginning of the human race with all the living, just people. To give a complete new start, the vessel also contained two samples of each type animal, and seven of each species that was suitable for food.

Therefore, it was necessary for all the past to be left behind. Lamech II died five years before the flood. Methuselah died immediately before the deluge began. Therefore, the complete family was in the Ark. What an exciting, complete plan!

Noah's name translates he shall comfort us. Lamech II attributed his personal toil or work with the curse on the ground. Noah was seen as a release from the struggle. It was revealed to Lamech II that Noah would be part of a great change.

Noah's family was the only moral people on the earth at this time. An ancient history record, the chronicles of Jasher, is referenced in Joshua and II Samuel. Jasher 5:15 identifies Noah's wife as Naamah. Noah fathered three sons, Japheth, Ham, and Shem. Then Noah took the three daughters of Eliakim, son of Methuselah, for wives for his sons (Jasher 5:35). These were cousins of the young men. Shem's bride was Sedeqetelebab.

Noah's three sons followed in the father's religion, tradition, and work. These would be the start of a new life, a new race, a new civilization. The tolerance and grace of a perfect Creator is revealed again.

We cannot foresee what is coming. We may not understand what is happening in our own lives. Nevertheless, there is always a bright future, if we have faith.

Favor in the eyes ─────────────

But Noah found favor in the eyes of the LORD. Was Noah infallible? No. Was Noah better than other men? Probably. Is perfection necessary for grace? Absolutely not. Repeatedly, throughout the canon, we find that mortal, fallible men obtain favor.

> But Noah found grace in the eyes of the LORD.
> - Genesis 6:8

He walked with God. His principles were based on the true, moral precepts of the Creator.

Noah trained his progeny to walk in the right way. They followed his values even during the time there was evil all around. This is perhaps the greatest legacy a man can have. All his children walked in his footsteps. Were they without mistakes? No, but like their father, they based their decisions on proper values.

The end of all flesh is come before me, clearly states the Creator's displeasure.

> And God said unto Noah, The end of all flesh is come before me;
> - Genesis 6:13

The breathing creatures of the earth would be pulled down or devastated. The term does not mean completely wiped-out, but rather wounded or killed. The destruction would allow a residual for rebuilding. Specifically, all air-breathing animals would be decimated.

> And, behold, I, even I, do bring a flood of waters upon the earth, to destroy all flesh, wherein is the breath of life, from under heaven; and every thing that is in the earth shall die.
> - Genesis 6:17

Noah became the man with the plan. He was instructed specifically to make an ark. The specifications look like an engineer prepared the plans.

How do you destroy an area, but protect a remnant? A shelter provides refuge from the holocaust. Ark is from the Latin, which means to shut-up or enclose. Although it is a place of refuge, because of environmental considerations it had to float. However, by current standards, it would not be considered a boat since it was not powered and not navigable.

Father of us all ━━━━━━━━━

After the flood, the vessel settled on the mountains of Ararat.

> And the ark rested in the seventh month, on the seventeenth day of the month, upon the mountains of Ararat (780).
> - Genesis 8:4

The same word Ararat (780) is also translated as Armenia (780). The area is in the northeast corner of present day Turkey. Note this verse is from the only two identical chapters of the record.

> And it came to pass, as he was worshipping in the house of Nisroch his god, that Adrammelech and Sharezer his sons smote him with the sword; and they escaped into the land of Armenia (780):
> - Isaiah 37:38 & II Kings 19:37

Noah's family left Ararat in Armenia and migrated to the southeast. They met the Tigris and Euphrates Rivers and traveled down toward the Persian Gulf. The rivers provided direction, an easy path, water, food, and protection. Without outside influences, this was a reasonable progress for the tribe.

Historically, the Tigris and Euphrates valley has been considered the cradle of civilization. Traditional archaeology has traced the roots of all the major cultures to this region. This correlates well with the Genesis account.

The boat landing is at the top of the Fertile Crescent. The Fertile Crescent is anchored by Israel and the Mediterranean Sea on the west. It extends in an arc up through ancient Assyria. There, the crescent intercepts the headwaters of the Tigris and Euphrates rivers. These then extend across ancient Babylon to the Persian Gulf.

The family traveled and settled in the plain of Shinar, located in modern Iraq. Apparently, Noah in time made his home on the gulf coast at Fara, according to the tradition of Josephus. The deposits from the river deltas have filled in the upper end of the gulf. Therefore, the settlements are now about 200 miles inland.

After the flood, all the earth was populated from Noah's sons, Shem, Ham, and Japheth. Rather than race, perhaps the easiest way to categorize people groups is by language. From this family came the major language groups. This is obvious if the name of the descendants is allocated to the countries the people founded.

People lived for almost 1000 years. Their childbearing age was hundreds of years. Therefore, in a very few generations, a large number of people would result.

Why the tree ━━━━━━━

Why would this family list be given in such detail? The early genealogy is common for all the descendants on the planet. After the time of the separation of the land and languages, only one family is carried through. This is the royal family of the Messiah.

The list is uniquely accurate and complete. There is no parallel in other histories. Those generally are restricted to a report about only their culture.

This record gives the relationship of all cultures. Other histories begin with a mythological story. This record is about a family that has been preserved through time.

Since mankind had a common beginning, there was a common language at this time. The next episode will address the family line up to a separation because of language.

Review ────────────

List the patriarchs associated with each situation.

1. The first recorded man.
2. The son born after the first death.
3. A man who never died, but was translated.
4. The oldest man in history.
5. The man who lived 777 years and was cut short.
6. The architect of the ark.
7. The three sons who built the ark.
8. The typical lifespan before the deluge was almost how many years?

12

GENEALOGY 201 - LINGUISTICS

Thought
The gift of life sure beats the alternative.

History repeats ━━━━━━━━━━━

This episode is the second in the series about the human lineage of the Messiah. The previous chapter looked at the patriarchs up to the deluge during the era of Noah. This section will look at the explosive growth of the human family up to the separation of languages. The next chapter follows the Semitic family through the line of the King. In addition, this chapter provides affirmation of the validity of the Old Testament account through correlations to other records and ancient histories.

Where did the messianic family live after the flood?

> And the whole earth was of one language and one speech. And it came to pass, as they journeyed from the east, that they found a plain in the land of Shinar; and they dwelt there.
> - Genesis 11:1

After the Noah family departed from the mountains, they traveled down the Euphrates. They then settled in Shinar and built Babel. Babel was in its zenith during Noah's lifetime.

Babel is onomatopoeia, a word that sounds like what it means. Babel is used to describe the noise a baby makes. The name of the city has become associated with confusion after the separation of the languages.

Human government ━━━━━━━━━━

Noah's grandson Nimrod was premier of the city of Babel according to Genesis 10. The *Septuagint*, the traditional Greek translation of the Hebrew *Torah*, called him a giant. He evidently carried dominant genes from the people described in Genesis 6. The account also says he challenged God. That rebellion was part of the Babel debacle.

Mythology has fables about giants that built mountains to challenge the gods. The gods then came and blew away the monuments. Mythology is stories that were often based on facts but were altered by various telling of the tales.

Nimrod was regarded as a mighty hunter. This is significant since the term had not been used up to this time. Various writers have attempted to infer the significance of the word hunter *(tsayid, 6718)*. In addition to its traditional meaning, it is often used for one who preys on another. It can range from murder to only oppression. History shows that most kingdoms are established and maintained by the abuse of people.

The beginning of his kingdom is the first reference to human government. Before this time, a patriarch who maintained family values and integrity managed the clans or tribes. Establishment of a city kingdom removed the family responsibility and authority. A new common authority, the king, replaced family structure.

Archaeology and history ━━━━━━━━━━

Numerous ancient historians and tablets record the events of the tower of Babel. Herodotus saw the tower and described it. A

Targum was an Aramaic translation of portions of the Old Testament. The *Targums of Jonathan ben Uzziel* and *Targums of Jerusalem* declare the tower was for idolatrous worship. Nebuchadnezzar restored and beautified the tower, and it was dedicated to the sun god, Bel.

It is unnecessary to use secular events to verify the Scriptural accounts. However, critics often try to discredit the religious record as unscientific or myths. When archaeology and other recorded history have related accounts, it can be used as correlation.

Notice the etymology between the god's name and the name of the city. Bel was also the god of fertility and sexual expression. His worship often involved licentious acts. A later chapter will deal with him and other false gods.

Because of their impious religious practices, the city fell into ruins. The clans separated into different regions. According to tradition, the patriarch Noah for some time lived at Fara. It is located in the delta between the Tigris and Euphrates. Noah is also linked with Fo Hi (Fu Hsi) or Yao, the first emperor of China, as well as the patriarch of other societies.

People were scattered from the city of Babel. However, the site was not abandoned. A latter group rebuilt the area to the south as Babylon. Babylon then progressed to become one of the long-term world empires. Present day Baghdad on the Tigris River is only 50 miles away from ancient Babylon.

The boys

From the three sons of Noah, we are given a clue about the different language groups. Care must be exercised to prevent creating a caste or class from these concepts. Individuals are unique. However, we have certain features and characteristics from our heritage. We also have certain tendencies because of our environment. History has borne out the tendencies given to the patriarchs of the language groups.

Japheth has been translated as enlarge. This is appropriate since this group has developed into the dominant language structure. They tend to be the science and technological leaders, who think in the abstract.

Shem has been translated to mean simply name or more eloquently renown. This is appropriate since the group fathered much of the great religious influence of the world. They tend to be oriented to finance and trade.

Ham has been translated to mean sun burnt or swarthy. This group tends to be the artisans and craftsmen with very practical skills. In addition, they were the early travelers around much of the globe before the later Indo-European historians made their travels.

All these gentlemen were from one language family. Each child born in a family has unique gifts and abilities. Similarly, these three patriarchs fostered unique tendencies. However, be cautious, the language groups are global not local or regional.

Shem, Ham, and Japheth

Linguists divide languages into three major classifications - Semitic, Hamitic, and Japhetic. The language groups correspond to the descendants of Noah and the areas they settled. The Semitic languages are primarily located in southwestern Asia in the area of the Middle East. These include Assyrian, Aramaic, Hebrew, and Arabic.

The Hamitic languages are located in Africa and East Asia. These include Coptic, ancient Libyan, modern Berber, and Cushitic of east Africa. It includes several of the Oriental and Pacific clans.

The Japhetic language has been called the Indo-European. This includes the Indian sub-continent as well as most of the European languages.

The families migrated into different regions. A person's mother tongue is the language of emotions. It is the language used for childhood communication and seems to become part of the personality. Without close communications, the languages would naturally be isolated into more dialects. When the dialects were adequately separated, new languages appeared.

Several tables are proposed to illustrate the spread of the people and the resulting languages. These are from the best information available at this time. Those cultures that linguists and historians have some agreement on are noted. Other authorities have made different judgments for a few names and locations. Nevertheless, the variations are not adequate to create fundamental changes in understanding.

No historian can absolutely affirm he has the total information, since the data is by necessity gathered after the fact. However, ancient recorded histories back to Noah are found in numerous societies including China, Iran, India, Scandinavia, and Britain.

All people of the world trace their history to his sons. What is intriguing is the dates of these records are phenomenally similar considering they are cross-cultural and from diverse parts of the world. These cannot be considered derivatives since the accounts predate Judeo-Christian contact and often have contrary ethics.

As would be expected, the migration of the East is less well-known in Western history. The common names to Western culture are based on the Greek, but these were sometimes distorted. The monikers were spelled and pronounced differently in their respective tongues and changed when translated.

The original groups were people who had direct contact with each other. Note also that after the first generation, the names are actually tribes rather than individuals. For example, words ending in *ite* are a people group and words ending in *im* indicate plurals. Some of these people groups have merged or passed from active usage. As a result, it is sometimes difficult to determine the current corresponding language and area.

Where did the big group go ▬▬▬▬▬▬▬

The progeny of Japheth formed the major European and south Asian subcontinent contingent identified in Table 1. Languages reflect family systems. Gentiles reflect people of the same gens, clan, or race. It is used to indicate foreigners to the Hebrews.

One location for part of the Japhetic tribe was the isles of the Gentiles. The location has caused some conjecture. Certain authors think it refers to the various nations. Others think it may actually refer to islands. Particularly it is sometimes assumed to refer to the British Isles and the isles of the Mediterranean.

The Japhetic people were explorers, conquerors, and developers. Part of the tribe eventually established a long history in Iran and the India sub-continent. The major branch of the tribe formed the great Western civilizations. These people have dominated world history for the past two thousand years. These groups can generally be divided into the three categories of Table 2.

Table 1: Japheth Countries

Son	Area	Progeny	Area
Gomer	Cimmeria	Togarmah	Asia Minor, Europe, Armenia
		Riphath	Paphlagonia, Galatia, Celt, Gael, Cimbri/Jute
		Askenaz	Rhegini, Scythia, Norse, Teuton
Magog			N. Black Sea, Ukraine, some Scythia
Medai / Shen-Nung	Medes		Northwest Iran, India
		Ian / Yan	Chiang of China
Javan	Ionia	Elishah	Greece, Aeoli, Elysian Fields, Alanus, Brutus/Bretons
		Tarshish	Spain, Atlantic Coast
		Kittim	Cyprus
		Dodanim	Dardanelle
Tubal	Tabali		Iberia/Georgia, Tobolsk
Meshech	Mushki		Russia, Slav
Tiras	Aegea		Tyrsenoi (Etruscans)

Table 2: Japheth Languages

Language Sub group	Derivatives
Eastern SubContinent	Iranian - Indian - Armenian
Southern Europe	Greek - Latin (Romance) - Albanian
Northern Europe	Germanic - Celtic - Slavic

The Breton history by Nennius includes Noah - Japheth - Javan - Iobaath and so on to Alanus, the father of Western Europe. One of his sons Hisicion sired Brutus, who was the first Breton in 1104 BC. This predates the establishment of the first king in Israel.

One Norse history links Sceaf or Seskaf to Japheth. However, the ages do not add. It appears that Sceaf lived as recent as 100 BC.

The political subdivisions of countries often contain many cultural clans. In addition, names change. Therefore, the following correlations may be helpful: Gauls - French, Gaels - Scots, Celts - Irish, Goths - Germans, and Bretons - Welsh.

With the technological explosion of the past century, the entire planet is now under the influence of a single Japhetic clan. The English language has become the trade language of the world. English is a German derivative language through several paths in the line of Gomer, the son of Japheth. Because of the Norman Conquest in 1066, English also has French influence derived from Latin in the line of Javan from Japheth. This seems to be a fulfillment of Noah's blessing to Japheth that he would be enlarged.

It is fascinating to see the rise and fall of the civilizations. Each has its unique ability, culture, and day in history.

Where did the other travelers go? ━━━━━━━

The sons of Ham also migrated from the homeland of Babel. This language group takes some most unusual twists. These people traveled south into Africa and east into Asia. The modern derivatives are fascinating as shown in Table 3.

Table 3: Ham Countries

Son	Grandson	Progeny	Area
Cush	Seba		Sabea, Ethiopia
	Havilah		E. Arabic coast
	Sabtah		Sabaten, India
	Raamah	Sheba, Dedan	UAE
	Sabtecha		Yeman, America?
	Nimrod	Babel, Erech, Accad, Calah	Shinar & Ninevah
	Seddiya		Polynesia
Mizraim	Ludim		N. Africa
	Ananim		N. Africa
	Lehabim		N. Africa
	Naphtuhim		N. Africa
	Pathrusim		Pathros
	Casluhim	Philistim	Palestine
	Caphtorim		N. Africa
Put	10 others		Libya, Cyrene
	Huang Di		China emperor
Canaan	Sidon		Phoenicia
	Heth/Hittite		Turkey, Cathay
	Jebus		ancient Jerusalem
	Amorite +5		Sinai Peninsula
	Arkite		Phoenicia
	Sinite		Sino/China

Again, the exact location and relationship between some of the dialects is not precisely known. Many of the languages did not maintain recorded script until recent years. The approximate relationship of these groups is cataloged in Table 4.

Dynasties ━━━━━━━━━━━━

Archaeology provides many cases of kingdoms and dynasties established by the Hamitic line. Assyrian and Babylonian empires, the city-state of Ninevah, and the long run dynasty of Egypt are examples. In early times, Semitic people overran many of these Asian and African societies, with the notable exception of Egypt. In

Table 4: Ham Languages

Son	Language	Sub	Area
Cush	Hottentot		S. Africa
	Bantu	Swahili	E. Africa
	Congo, Philippines, Sudan, East Indies		
Mizraim	Coptic		N. Africa
Canaan (Heth)	Altaic	Ottoman	Turkey
		Mongolia	N. China
	Uralic	Finland, Hungary, Estonia, Siberia	Scattered Huns

addition, in other areas around the world, the Japhetic people overran the Hamitic clans who were already there, and their culture was devastated. That is the nature of changing societies.

Secular history verifies that civilization first developed in the Chaldean region of the Fertile Crescent. The culture continued to flourish in the form of the Babylonian dynasties. After the separation of the clans, the Hamitic culture made a parallel development in Egypt. Archaeological excavations illustrate the contemporary relationship of the two great societies and religions.

The home boys ━━━━━━━━━━━

The son Shem had the smallest family. This group remained in the area in which the family had settled. The other two groups traveled. However, part of the Hamitic family stayed nearby in the region. These became intertwined with part of the Semitic family.

The relationship between Shem and Semitic is simply a different pronunciation in northern and southern Hebrew. The only difference in the two spellings is a single dot that differentiates the letters *sin* and *shin*.

Shem was the great grandfather of Eber. Eber means the other side or across. It may refer to those beyond the river Euphrates or the archaeology site Habiru. His name was used to identify the language of the Hebrews.

Table 5: Shem Countries

Son	2	3	4	5	Area
Elam					Sushan, E. Persian Gulf
Assur					Assyria
Arphaxad	Shelah	Eber	Peleg	Reu	Chaldea, N.E. Ninevah
			Jokthan	11 other	Semitic Arab tribes
				Havilah	Tibet
				Jobab	Tang then Shang of China
					Jesharelah / Hou Chi then Chou of China
Lud					Lydia
Aram	Uz				Aramaea, S. Damascus
	Hul				Armenia
	Gether				Bactria
	Mash				Charax Spasini

This family tree has the most information since it is repeated in several accounts of the anthology. However, it never grew to the size of the other clans. Most of these locations and language groups are well known since a written language was maintained. Again, the language group can be categorized by the later derivatives.

Many scholars argue that the original, common language was Chaldean and similar to Hebrew. Although that cannot be verified, it is a reasonable expectation. The Hebrew language was maintained in use until the demise of the nation of Israel and the dispersion of the people about 150 AD, under the Roman Empire. The language was fast becoming a dead language. It was only maintained in written form and by merging with other tongues such as Chaldean and Yiddish, which is a mix of Hebrew with German.

As various empires took over the Middle East, their languages were used in the region. Eliezer Ben-Yehuda resurrected Hebrew in the early twentieth century. It was restored to common use when the

Table 6: Shem Languages

Language Sub group	Derivatives
East Semitic	Akkadian, Babylonian, Assyrian
North West Semitic	Phoenician, Punic, Aramaic, Hebrew
South West Semitic	Arabic, Ethiopic, Amharic.

nation of Israel was reestablished in 1948.

The authority for the country was decreed by the United Nations under influence by the United States and Britain to decolonize the region. Since it was recent history to us, our elementary school teachers discussed the resurrection of the language and the country.

All for one and one for all ─────────────

It is fascinating that modern linguistics organize language structures in three major categories. These even use the name of the sons of Noah. The structure of languages gives further credence to the accuracy of the chronicle. These languages and family relationships divide all the people of the earth from a common start.

The beauty and order of languages should provoke an appreciation of the human condition. The sounds of a foreign language appear as incoherent noise. However, the mother tongue is music to the ear of a listener. Cacophony (disharmony) to one is elegant order to another.

The hand of an overriding power is so readily apparent in language. The order and recognition of a shared thread points to a common beginning. The Hebrew journal is the most rational explanation for this phenomenal characteristic.

Pangaea ─────────────

Peleg, a great-great grandson, was born during the lifetime of Noah. His name simply means to divide. The chronicles affirm that during his days the earth was divided. It is generally claimed that comment refers to the separation of the language groups at Babel.

> Two sons were born to Eber: One was named Peleg, because in his time the earth was divided;
> - Genesis 10:25

That provides one theory for population on all the continents. It also explains why similar records of civilization are around the world. These include stories, myths, religious practices, and ancient architecture. Compare the Inca culture of South America with the Egyptian culture of the Nile. These are very similar and appear to be almost contemporary.

Is there a complementary possibility? There is general agreement among scientists that all the landmass of the earth was once connected. This super continent was called Pangaea. Then the earth began shifting and separating in a process called plate tectonics. The earth plates moving further apart would explain some historical phenomenon.

The Middle East is the intersection of some of the most active tectonic regions of the earth. In other areas, the present rate of motion for the North Atlantic is at 1.25 inches per year. The East Pacific region is moving at 7" per year. These rates are not constant, but indicate the dynamic nature of the Earth's crust.

Others contend the separation of Pangaea would have occurred much earlier. This could have been a result of the inundation of the continent. However, the name description appears unique and the circumstances of a global migration tend to fit a later severance of the landmass.

Time and again

Dates of archaeological events are subject to substantial inference. These are generally based on the type of pottery or other implements found during excavations. If a written record is found with the implements, it may be correlated to a similar event in another culture. This circuitous method leaves considerable room for variations in time. Besides, societies seldom record events associated with other cultures, unless it is a victory over them.

An era or age is used to describe the archaeological layers. The earliest is the Neolithic age, which contained only stone implements. There were metal implements used by the Cain civilization prior to the flood. However, different clans that live during the same time would obviously not have the same lifestyle and tools. All these variations add to the difficulty of establishing dates. Equally professional archaeologists and anthropologists will set dates hundreds to thousands of years apart.

The earliest verifiable dates are approximately 2000 BC in every major culture. Any dates prior to this time are selected based on the perspective of the numerologist. Recent archaeological research tends to point to findings back as much as 10,000 to 50,000 years. Regardless of the technique, that is still relatively recent history.

Another point of consternation is the length of time recorded in various translations. For example, the Greek *Septuagint* uses somewhat different numbers for the years of Shem's descendants. Further, at various times, the years have been calculated on a different basis, such as king dates. Because of the divergence, no theology should be built on the dates. Nevertheless, they can provide insight into the sequence of events. The relationships between people can also be discerned.

Conscientious theologians and archaeologists explain the accounts, explain away the time accounts, or accept them as factual. An independent council developed the longest surviving English translation, the Authorized Version. The King authorized and provided for the council. These gentlemen of dissimilar heritage came to agreement. The consensus was based on the evaluation of numerous earlier records. The process gives as much credibility to the translation as can be reasonably expected. This is not to discredit other good works with different genealogical times. There has been extensive archaeology developed in the four hundred years since that translation.

Because it is so common, several observations can be made about the commonly translated dates. Again, these are intriguing, but no special insight or practices should be built on this information.

The ages of the early patriarchs are shown in Table 7. The year of the world origin is *Anno Mundi (AM)* from Latin. The year of birth is calculated from this start of time. The beginning is based on the initiation of Adam. The age of the father at the birth of his succeeding son is recorded. The age at demise is also reported. The year of his demise is calculated from the initial era. All these data are based on the Authorized Version.

A tabulation of the date of birth is also represented in BCE. These dates are derived from the times calculated by an Irish scholar, Archbishop James Ussher, in 1650 AD.

Table 7: Patriarch Ages

#	Patriarch	Born about BCE	Born year AM	Had next son at age of	Age expired	Expired year AM
1	Adam	4004	0	130	930	930
2	Seth	3874	130	105	912	1042
3	Enosh	3769	235	90	905	1140
4	Kenan	3679	325	70	910	1235
5	Mahalalel	3609	395	65	895	1290
6	Jared	3544	460	162	962	1422
7	Enoch	3382	622	65	365	987
8	Methuselah	3317	687	187	969	1656
9	Lamech	3130	874	182	777	1651
10	Noah	2948	1056	500	950	2006
11	Shem	2448	1556	100	600	2156
12	Arphaxad	2348	1656	35	438	2094
13	Shelah	2313	1691	30	433	2124
14	Eber	2283	1721	34	464	2185
15	Peleg	2249	1755	30	239	1994
16	Reu	2219	1785	32	239	2024
17	Serug	2187	1817	30	230	2047
18	Nahor	2157	1847	29	148	1995
19	Terah	2128	1876	70	205	2081
20	Abraham	2058	1946	100	175	2121
21	Isaac	1958	2046	60	180	2226

His treatise on chronology has proved quite durable, even if debatable. It was based on an elaborate correlation between Mediterranean and Middle Eastern histories and ancient Scripture. It was incorporated into an Authorized Version of the Bible in 1701.

As such, this numeration is based on language information, rather than physical artifacts. There have been substantial discoveries in archaeology, ethnology, and history since that time. Much of it correlates to the estimates, but some have very different results.

Even if Ussher's initial date of 4004 BC is off somewhat, the sequence of times appear to be reasonably valid and generally fits archaeological dating processes. An error of 10% in time either way would only shift some dates by about 600 years. That actually is quite close for such tentative data.

All calendars have some variations, since there have been many adjustments over the eons. In addition, virtually all calendars are based on either the solar cycle, the lunar or Metonic cycle of the Greeks, or the Roman indiction or tax cycle. The solar cycle is 28 years, the Metonic cycle is 19 years, and the Roman indiction is 15 years. Therefore, correlations are tedious at best.

If there were no changes, the cyclic convergence of these would be (28 x 19 x 15) = 7980 years. A French mathematician Joseph Justus Scaliger developed the Julian period and correlated the cycles to have an initial time of *Anno Mundi* at 4713 BC. With all the variations, this is definitely within range of Ussher's dates. Again, too much should not be made of the age calculations.

Coming of age ─────────────────

A very interesting pattern is noted in the ages of the patriarchs. Prior to the deluge, all people lived about the same length of time. At the inundation, the life expectancy was cut in half. There is another slice in half after the separation of the people. The next reduction by half was before the time of Moses, when the span became 120 years.

Before the deluge, this was set as the projected life expectancy of the human race. There is no apparent reason that people cannot live to this age.

> Then the LORD said, my Spirit will not contend with man forever, for he is mortal; his days will be a hundred and twenty years.
> - Genesis 6:3 NIV

Nevertheless, life expectancy continued to deteriorate to the steady value of about seventy years. The condition had been reached before 1000 BC, when the king recorded his observation.

> The days of our years are threescore years and ten; and if by reason of strength they be fourscore years, yet is their strength labor and sorrow; for it is soon cut off, and we fly away.
> - Psalm 90:10

This pattern of decay in life expectancy exactly matches the exponential solution of the triad equation of time discussed earlier. The result is additional indication that the sequence of dates has validity.

Mythology and Melchizadek ────────────

Noah had no children after the flood. He was 600 years old when the deluge began and was 601 years old when the waters dried up. History asserts he lived 350 years after the flood. The elapsed time to each new generation is given as well as the total life span of the patriarch.

> And Noah lived after the flood three hundred and fifty years. And all the days of Noah were nine hundred and fifty years: and he died.
> - Genesis 9:28-29

Shem was the father of all the Semitic people that were born. He lived for 502 years after the inundation and fathered many children. Tradition avows that he was Melchizedek, the person who was called the ancient of days without beginning or ending. Notice he came out of the flood and he outlived the next nine generations, with the exception of Eber. That would make him appear immortal.

Another brother, Japheth, became a god in the history and mythology of many Europeans. His name was slightly different in the various cultures, but close inspection shows the trend. The Romans called him Jove or Japater, which transliterates to Jupiter. To the Greeks, he was Iapheth. In two India societies, he was Prajapaty and Jyapeti. To the Turks he was Yafith. In Israel, he was Joffa. To the Saxons he was Iafeth.

The third brother, Ham, became a god of the African culture. Tradition claims he was the father of the first Egyptian Pharaoh and his wife established the worship system in that civilization. Pharaohs were regarded as both monarchs and gods. The first Pharaoh was apparently Menes, also called Narmer.

One family only ───────────

Genesis 10 records the complete human race divergence. We have shown there is substantial historical and archaeological correspondence to these events. Even a monotheistic God was in many societies around the world that have the early records.

Genesis 10 is the last chapter to deal broadly with the entire human race. Chapter 11 gives the background for the separation and the direction of the Semitic clans. After the separation of the people, language began to change. Diverse cultures developed and various religious influences infiltrated the lifestyles.

A single language family is the focus of the remainder of the preserved writ. This is not surprising. If people were isolated and used different languages, it would be impractical to expect a common history. The recorded history is that of the Hebrew language family.

Was God completely absent from the other peoples? Is it possible there is a parallel religious history in another language? Are the other religious traditions as valid as the Hebrew? These have been questions and the foundations for many diverse religious and philosophical systems. Many of the account's responses are identified in this ancient record.

Review

Identify the following people.

1. Son of Noah that moved north.
2. Son of Noah that settled the Middle East.
3. Son of Noah that fathered Africa and the Orient.
4. The leader of the Babel culture.
5. What was the god of Babel?
6. According to tradition, who was Melchizedek?

13

GENEALOGY 301 - ROYALTY

Thought
There is always a price to pay.
There is a price for success.
There is a price for failure.

A new celebrity ─────────

This third and final chapter of genealogy relates to the family tree. The lineage now focuses into one ethnic group.

One of the amazing observations is that all the major progenitors were very fallible. Numerous had sexual infidelities. That caused substantial problems for them and their families. Nevertheless, the perfect man came from this line.

Another phenomenon is related to the Middle Eastern culture. In that environment, the first-born son inherits the family fortune and title. However, the Messianic line did not always remain in the first-born line. The first four generations from Abraham were not from the oldest son. Even the line of the king progressed outside of this first son pattern.

Leaving Chaldea ─────────

Moving on down the family tree, Terah was the eighth generation after Shem. The other generations listed only the progenitor. The

ETHNIC LINE
Shem
Arphaxad
Salah
Eber
Peleg
Reu
Serug
Nahor
Terah
Abraham
Isaac
Jacob
Judah
Pharez
Esrom
Aram
Amminadab
Nahshon
Salmon
Boaz
Obed
Jesse
David

chronicle changes with Terah. All three of his sons are identified. His heirs were Abram, Nahor, and Haran. The family of these guys forms the keystone of the remainder of the Genesis annals. From Genesis the story goes on to the King.

Haran predeceased his father. Nevertheless, a city-state was named for Haran. He had a daughter Milcah who married his brother Nahor. He also had a son Lot, who would become a central player in the family of Abram.

Abram's wife was Sarai. There is affirmation she was the daughter of his father, but not his mother.

> And yet indeed she is my sister; she is the daughter of my father, but not the daughter of my mother; and she became my wife.
> - Genesis 20:12

Josephus, the ancient secular historian, further affirms she was the sister of Milcah and Lot. This would still fit the language of Genesis. Hence, she was a half-sister or more likely the niece of Abram. Sarai, a most notable lady, was barren until she was 90 years old.

Terah began a migration from Ur of Chaldea up the Tigris and Euphrates Rivers toward Canaan. He took Abram, Abram's wife Sarai, and his grandson Lot. Notwithstanding, the journey came to a halt in Haran (Padanaram) where Terah died.

A new dispensation

Using the dates given in the common English chronicle, Abram was born 292 years after the flood. If this is the case, Noah was still alive at that time. He was living in the same area of Ur of Chaldea. As the forebear of all living people, Noah undoubtedly had substantial influence.

Abram's name was changed to Abraham, which means the father of many nations or people. In a similar vein, his spouse's name was changed from Sarai to Sarah. With Abraham, the dispensation of relations to the Almighty changed from the flood mentality of Noah.

Abraham continued the migration into Canaan that his father had started. There he built an altar to God. He was given a promise of inheritance for that country. His migration continued on to Egypt. He allowed the king to take Sarah to be one of his wives. The relationship was never consummated because of numerous conflicts. Regardless of the peccadillo between his wife and the king of that country, he became a man of tremendous wealth.

Abraham took his wife and nephew Lot back to Canaan. He became a huge rancher with a large staff. Nevertheless, he did not have an heir.

At eighty-six years old, he felt he might have to leave his empire to a servant. In an agreement with his wife, he fathered a child with a young maid Hagar from the Ham lineage. This first-born son was Ishmael.

When he was 99 and Sarah was 89, they were promised a son by a theophany, a physical manifestation of God. In the next year, a young son, Isaac, was born. He received the promise of the father's inheritance in land and the Messianic line.

Conflict developed between the two boys. Sarah forced Abraham to send Hagar and her son away from the home. However, we find later that they did not travel far.

Ishmael married and fathered 12 sons. These became the fathers of major segments of Arabic culture. Their claim to the inheritance of the land of their father, Abraham, is based on the first-born rights. This conflict continues to this day in the Middle East.

After Sarah passed to the next life, Abraham took another wife, Keturah from the Japheth lineage. She gave him six sons, although he was very old at the time. The sons of Keturah were not regarded in any of Abraham's inheritance.

> Then again Abraham took a wife, and her name was Keturah. And she bare him Zimran, and Jokshan, and Medan, and Midian, and Ishbak, and Shuah.
> - Genesis 25:1-2

Abraham passed on at 175 years of age. Abraham was buried in the cave of Machpelah that he had bought for his wife Sarah. His first-born son, Ishmael, and the son of his inheritance, Isaac, took care of the final rest for their father.

Isaac ⸻

Abraham sent an emissary to his homeland to obtain a wife for his son Isaac. He found Rebecca, the daughter of Bethuel, Nahor's son, whom Milcah bore unto him. From our earlier observation, Rebecca was a cousin of Isaac.

Like his father, Isaac allowed the same peccadillo between his wife and the king. Nevertheless, the marriage was protected.

Rebecca had twins, Esau and Jacob. Esau, the oldest, sacrificed his inheritance to his brother for a bowl of soup. When he recovered his senses, he was very angry. To add insult to injury, Jacob stole the family blessing from his father through trickery.

In the culture, the oldest son would inherit the major portion of the family fortune. He would become the new patriarch of the family business. This inheritance was called the birthright.

In addition, the father would proclaim a blessing on the sons. This blessing was his vision of the potential of the progeny. It was a verbal proclamation for the success of the heir. Because of the birthright, the oldest son generally received the proclamation of prosperity. Nevertheless, the father could announce a blessing on the other children.

Much to his parents' chagrin, Esau married a daughter of the family of Ishmael. His offspring became the clan Edom, which is later translated Idumea.

This line was not in the king line. Nevertheless, we find one of the most powerful rulers was from this area. Herod, King during the birth of Jesus, was from Idumea. Hence, we see the long-term impact of a family action. We also see why King Herod was so uptight when the wise men asked about the birth of the King.

Jacob ─────────────────

Rebecca wanted to protect Jacob and to keep him from marrying outside the clan. Therefore, Isaac sent him to his mother's brother Laban.

Jacob fell in love with Laban's younger daughter Rachael. He worked for 7 years to earn her hand in marriage. However, Laban tricked him and gave the older daughter, Leah, on the wedding night. As was then common, Laban also gave him Zilpah as a maid for Leah.

After one week, he was given his true love, Rachael. Then, he had to work another 7 years to pay the endowment for his enamored favorite. Again, he was also given a maid, Bilhah, for Rachael.

Jacob fathered 12 sons by the four women. The first-born was Reuben by Leah. Leah gave him three more sons. Her fourth was Judah. Much in contrast to tradition, Judah became the king line.

Jacob developed a huge fortune while in Chaldea. He began a return to the homeland of his father, Isaac. On the way, he encountered an angel of the LORD *(Yehovah)*. After a struggle with the angel, Jacob was injured in the thigh. Because of this event, his name was changed to Israel.

> And he said, Your name shall be called no more Jacob, but Israel:
> for you have striven with God and with men, and have prevailed.
> - Genesis 32:28 ASV

Israel became the name of the clan and the country. His twelve sons became the fathers of the twelve tribes of the nation Israel. Note the similarity with the 12 tribes of Ishmael. This is another point in the contention between the Israeli and Arabic nations.

Judah ────────────────

Judah, like other ancestors, fathered sons by many different women. Judah was also called Zera. After some time, his oldest son Er married Tamar. Unfortunately, Er was killed while still a young man.

In the ancient tradition, a brother was obligated to marry the widow. The offspring of the union would be allocated to the deceased brother. Judah promised that his young son, Shelah, would marry Tamar when he was mature. In the interim, Tamar returned to her father's house.

When the young man was grown, Judah did not keep his promise. In the process of time, Judah's wife had passed from this life. After that, Tamar took the attire of a prostitute and went to Judah. He did not recognize that she was his former daughter-in-law. Judah liked what he saw and slept with her.

Tamar became pregnant from the tryst and she bore twins from the union. The first to stick his hand out was Zarah. The midwife tied a scarlet thread around his hand. This was the indication of the rights of the firstborn. The hand withdrew and Pharez was born. Apart from tradition, the second from the birth, Pharez, became the father of the king line.

From Egypt ────────────────

The entire family of Israel migrated to Egypt because of a famine in the land. The clan continued to grow while residing in the foreign turf. The sequence of the family line follows in staccato fashion.

Esrom was the son of Pharez. He fathered Aram, who gave Amminadab, who procreated Naason, from whom came Salmon.

The clan left Egypt under the leadership of Moses. Subsequently, Joshua became the general that led the crew across the Jordan River into the ancient homeland. Joshua sent two spies to check out the border city, Jericho.

The spies went into the house of a prostitute, Rahab. She protected the men and gave them help necessary for their survival. Later, when the army under Joshua overcame Jericho, Rahab and her father's family were given asylum with the new nation.

Salmon, also called Sala, married Rahab. Thus, the king line was narrowed through their son Boaz.

Kinsman redeemer ━━━━━━━━

Naomi, a lady from the family, married a man from another country, Moab. These are descendents from the illicit relationship between Lot and his daughter. Naomi traveled with her husband to Moab, his homeland. She had two sons, one who married a local lady, Ruth.

Naomi's husband and both sons departed this life. She decided to return home to the area around Jerusalem. Her daughter-in-law, Ruth, came back with her.

Their financial plight was very destitute. The family land had been foreclosed. Naomi told Ruth to glean from the fields of her near kinsman, Boaz. Ruth found favor with Boaz, and in the local tradition, went and slept under his cover with him. The next morning, he went to redeem the family heritage so he could marry Ruth.

The very last line of the story of Ruth reveals the relationship of Boaz to the kingship.

And Salmon begat Boaz, and Boaz begat Obed, and Obed begat
Jesse, and Jesse begat David.
- Ruth 4:21

The king has entered the building ─────────────

Little is known about Obed. However, we know his son Jesse had
seven sons. David was the youngest.

As a young man, David rocked the giant Goliath to sleep. Goliath
was the principal warrior for his nation, the Philistines. These were
descendents of the giant branch of Ham's family.

As a reward for destroying Goliath, David was married to King
Saul's daughter, Michal. The relationship provided no children. As
a very young man, David was also brought in as a general and
counselor to the king. That relationship proved to be tenuous at best
and hostile most of the time.

Eventually, David became the great monarch, who consolidated the
kingdom into the power of the day. During the interim, he had
married several other women.

> And David took him more concubines and wives out of Jerusalem,
> after he was come from Hebron: and there were yet sons and
> daughters born to David. And these be the names of those that were
> born unto him in Jerusalem; Shammua, and Shobab, and Nathan,
> and Solomon, Ibhar also, and Elishua, and Nepheg, and Japhia, and
> Elishama, and Eliada, and Eliphalet.
> - II Samuel 5:13-16

Nevertheless, as he was strolling about one evening, he saw a
gorgeous neighbor taking a bath. She was the wife of his friend and
general Urriah, a Hittite.

While her husband was out of town, David called Bathsheba over
for the evening. She became pregnant, so David arranged to have
his friend killed in battle. From this rendezvous, Bathsheba gave
birth to a son, who died in a few hours.

For his indiscretion, David was severely criticized by the prophet, Nathan. The King was told he would continue to have problems with his family because of the affair.

After this incident, Bathsheba became the Queen and gave David other sons. One, Solomon, was destined to be the King.

What an interesting character. David had more foibles than most men. Nevertheless, he was called a man after God's own heart.

> ...The LORD *(Yehovah)* has sought him a man after his own heart, and the LORD *(Yehovah)* has commanded him to be captain over his people...
> - I Samuel 13:14

This was not because of David's transgressions. Rather it was because of David's love for the principles of the Almighty.

Now the Messianic line takes two paths. One is through Solomon, the royal lineage. This will culminate in Joseph, the adoptive father of Jesus.

The other is through Nathan, the bloodline. This concludes with Joseph as the husband of Mary, who was the natural mother of Jesus.

ROYAL LINE

Solomon
Rehoboam
Abia
Asa
Jehosophat
Joram
Ahaziah
Joash
Amaziah
Uzziah
Joatham
Achaz
Hezekiah
Manasseh
Amon
Josiah
Jehoiakim
Jehoiakin
Salthiel
(via Pediah)
Zerubbabel
Abiud
Eliakim
Azor
Sadoc
Achim
Eliud
Eleazer
Matthan
Jacob
Joseph

The wisest man

Solomon consolidated the kingdom into the most powerful and peaceful nation of the day. He removed those of his father's advisers who were of questionable character. Rather than ask for wealth, Solomon implored God for wisdom. He became the wisest man who is recorded in history. With his reign came 40 years of peace and the greatest prosperity known to man.

With his power, he fulfilled every personal desire. One of those was his sensual appetite. He had over 300 wives and 600 mistresses. One must wonder how such a wise man could make such foolish choices in women.

The royals ━━━━━━━━━━━━━━

The son who inherited the kingdom was Rehoboam. In contrast to his grandfather and father, Rehoboam lost the major portion of the kingdom. He retained only the tribe of Judah and the tribe of Benjamin in the southern kingdom. The remaining 10 tribes formed the northern confederacy called Israel. That nation installed a new king, Jeroboam.

Most of the kings in both countries were unremarkable. One thing to note is the names are spelled differently in various accounts. The next generations after Rehoboam were Abia, then, Asa, then Josophat. He was followed by Joram. There the northern and southern kingdoms experienced a marriage between the children of the regents.

A particularly vile king of Israel, Ahab, had a very evil queen, Jezebel. Her name declares she was a priestess of the false god, Ba'al or Bel. Their daughter Athaliah was married to King Joram of Judah. This created a very traditional alliance between kingdoms.

Since the couple was very evil and depraved, their lineage was cursed for four generations. Therefore, the next three kings were omitted from the temple record. These were Ahaziah, Joash, and Amaziah. They are identified in the royal list by italics.

Ozias, also called Azariah and Uzziah, was the next in the recorded line. After Uzziah came Joatham, Achaz, Hezekiah, Manasseh, Amon, and Josiah. With the exception of Hezekiah, the above list of kings was less than spectacular.

Jehoiakim succeeded in the line. He is noted to have several brothers. He was the last king to come to the throne as a free man.

He unwisely aligned himself with Egypt and provoked the Babylonian regent. As a result, Nebuchanezzar overran the country and took him into captivity.

Johoiakim was reinstalled as a puppet king. He was so treacherous that his own subjects executed him by throwing him over the wall. He was cursed so his family would not rule the free throne of the nation.

His son was variously called Jehoiakin, Jeconiah, Jeconhias, Coniah, and Conias. Jehoiakin was regent for only three months when he provoked Nebuchadnezzar. He and his court were taken into captivity for 37 years.

There is a most unusual transition outside the royal line in conjunction with the bloodline. It is prudent to take a short overview of that family.

The family line ━━━━━━━━━━━

The family bloodline came from King David by way of his son Nathan. There is a list of normal, non-distinctive people.

Nevertheless, they had an important enough role to be listed in the most impressive history. These were Mattatha, Menan, Melea, Eliakim, Jonan, Joseph, Judah, Simeon, and Levi. Then came Matthat, Jorim, Eliezer, Jose, Er, Elmodam, Cosam, Addi, Melchi, and Neri.

The merger ━━━━━━━━━━━

Neri, in the bloodline, had a daughter who had a son Pediah. The daughter married Jehoiakin, in the royal line. Together they had several children including a son, Salthiel.

Salthiel was married, but demised before childbirth. According to custom, a brother was to take the childless widow. He would then bring up children for the departed. Hence, Salthiel's half-brother, Pediah apparently married his widow.

With this, the line of Jehoikim ended as forecast. However, the title of the kingship was legitimately passed on as if it were Salthiel's.

Hence, the royal line of David was actually perpetuated through the bloodline. This is important to the Messiah. His natural manhood came through the bloodline. Therefore, the actual relationship to King David was intact.

Zerubbabel was the descendent from this rather contorted merging of the lines. He also had a brother, Shimei. Zerubbabel is listed as the son of Salthiel in the royal line. He is also listed as the grandson of Neri in the bloodline. Both are legally correct. His name is in bold on both lists.

Zerrubabbel fathered two sons and a daughter, Shelomith. She married Rhesa. From that point, the family tree carries his name.

Royal line to Joseph ━━━━━━━━━━

This royal line never resided on the throne. It persisted through a series of not notable names. These were Abiud, Eliakim, Azor, Sadoc, Achim, Eliud, Eleazer, Matthan, and Jacob. The culmination was with Joseph, the husband of Mary.

Jesus was Joseph's legal son. Hence, he was entitled to the inheritance of the crown of King David. Throughout his adult ministry, he was frequently referred to by the epithet, Son of David.

FAMILY LINE
Nathan
Mattatha
Mainan
Melea
Eliakim
Jonan
Joseph
Juda
Simeon
Levi
Matthat
Jorim
Eliezer
Jose
Er
Elmodam
Cosam
Addi
Melchi
Neri
daughter
Shaltiel
Zerubbabel
Rhesa
Joanna
Juda
Joseph
Semei
Mattathias
Maath
Naggai
Esli
Naum
Amos
Mattathias
Joseph
Janna
Melchi
Levi
Matthat
Eli
Joseph

Bloodline to Mary ───────────

The bloodline came through Shelomith, the wife of Rhesa. The descendants were more numerous, but no more notable. These included Joanna, Juda, Joseph, Semei, Mattathias, Maath, Magge, Esli, and Nahum. They were followed by Amos, Mattathia, Joseph, Janna, Melchi, Levi, Matthat, and Heli.

Heli or Eli was apparently the father of Mary. In the early records the name of women were seldom used, but rather the name of the husband was recorded. That is not unlike ladies today taking on the family name of the husband.

Jesus received his natural bloodline through his mother Mary. The annals have traced his ancestry back to Adam. Another moniker that Jesus accepted in his ministry was the Son of Man.

Deity line of Father ───────────

The birth father of Jesus was God through the activity of the Spirit. This parental line makes the son be totally in the family of God and to be of God. That relationship provides the third autograph accepted by Jesus as the Son of Man.

Dispensation ───────────

Numerous eras were observed in investigating the heritage of the Messiah. These changes are often called dispensations. These are used to categorize the history of mankind and his relation to the Creator. A brief review of the periods of human understanding is in order.

1. The dispensation of Innocence lasted until the Eden travesty. The Creator was an active player.
2. The time of Conscience continued until the flood. Adam was the first inhabitant.

3. The era of Human Government endured until the migration. Noah was the focal authority.
4. The epoch of Promise covered the covenant with a new family. Abraham was the chief actor.
5. The age of Law transpired through the kings. Moses was the founder.
6. The period of the Church transcends human activity. Jesus was the architect.
7. The eons of the Kingdom will culminate the history.

What a fascinating exposé! Again, we have found that long term success comes only when the Creator is given preeminence. The enticing journal is profitable for our understanding and development.

Review

Complete each question.

1. What was the name of the language group to which the Messiah belongs?
2. Who is the Father of Promise and the Father of Faith?
3. Who was the prostitute that protected the spies and became great grandmother of the King?
4. Who was the great King of Israel?
5. Who was King David's paramour that became his wife?
6. Who was the wisest man and also King?
7. Who was the common descendant of the royal and the bloodline?

14

SPIRIT IS IN THE AIR

Thought
Faith is what you believe will happen.
Fear is what you believe will happen.
Only one is positive.
MOD

Third study ━━━━━━━━━━━

The Spirit is the third and final look at God. This mental, intellectual, rational member reflects the attitude of the Almighty.

...the thoughts of God no one knows except the Spirit of God.
- I Corinthians 2;11

And he that searches the hearts knows what is the mind of the Spirit...
- Romans 8:27

A short review of the other two studies is in order. In the Hebrew philosophy, the identities are not isolated. God, just as man, always has all three emotional, physical, and mental relationships involved. It is just that in our Western, Greek type rationale, we tend to categorize and isolate. Therefore, one characteristic appears stronger in some relationships. Hence during different eras of human history, one tends to dominate.

The first research was on the emotional will that is called God. In the analysis of that relationship, we looked at the names, attributes, and character traits. The emotional will was the predominant interaction between God and man during the Old Testament.

The second inquiry was into the physical person realizable with the senses. In the analysis, we looked at the names, ministry, and genealogy of Jesus, who formed the pivotal event of history. Traditional Western calendars were realigned to use the physical realization of God as the starting point. The duration of the physical identity was predominantly active for only 33 years.

The third study of God has moved into prominence and has remained there for two millennia. The mental faculty is the primary avenue to activity between God and man at this time.

Always there ━━━━━━━━━━━

From the beginning of creation to the end of the chronicles, the Spirit is involved.

> And the Spirit *(ruwach, 7307)* of God moved upon the face of the waters.
> - Genesis 1:2

> This is how the birth of Jesus Christ came about: His mother Mary was pledged to marry to Joseph, but before they came together, she was found to be with child through the Holy Spirit *(pneuma, 4151)*.
> - Matthew 1:18 NIV

> And the Spirit *(pneuma, 4151)* and the bride say, Come. And let him that hears say, Come. And let him that is thirsty come. And whosoever will, let him take the water of life freely.
> - Revelation 22:17

These references illustrate the range of activity of the Spirit. The mental capacity is actively concerned with every interaction between man and the Almighty.

Guiding ────────────

The Spirit is the intellect that guided the writing of the Scripture.

> For the prophecy came not in old time by the will of man: but holy
> men of God spoke as they were moved by the Holy Spirit.
> - II Peter 1:21

In the anthology, there were many authors with a variety of styles.
These writings occurred over a very long period, approximately
1500 years. The scribes came from different backgrounds,
educations, and cultures.

Regardless of the diversity of the authors, all the documents reflect
the same principles. The practices of the writers were many, but the
principles were consistent. This reliability is because of the unifying
intellectual influence of the Spirit. That is the reason the document
has lasted through over two thousand years.

Protector ────────────

When researching the Spirit of God, we find there are many actions.
In analyzing these verbs, it appears that one noun best expresses the
spectrum of ideas. The Spirit is around everything, so protector is an
excellent descriptor. In some circles the term Paraclete is used. That
simply means an advocate or intercessor.

As an illustration, look at some of the significant actions. Protector
covers all the bases.

> But the Comforter, which is the Holy Ghost, whom the Father will
> send in my name...
> - John 14:26

> ...the Holy Ghost, whom the Father will send in my name, he shall
> teach you all things...
> - John 14:26

And when they were come up out of the water, the Spirit of the
Lord caught away Philip...
- Acts 8:39

The Spirit itself bears witness with our spirit, that we are the
children of God:
- Romans 8:16

...but the Spirit itself makes intercession for us with groanings
which cannot be uttered.
- Romans 8:26

Who hath also sealed us, and given the earnest of the Spirit in our
hearts.
- II Corinthians 1:22

...in whom also after that ye believed, you were sealed with that
Holy Spirit of promise...
- Ephesians 1:13

Perhaps one of the most significant observations about the Spirit is
it never edifies itself, but always builds up the person of Jesus.

Positive attitude ━━━━━━━━━━

There are many spirits, but only one Holy Spirit. In a later chapter,
we will investigate various spirits in depth. For now, we will only
look at the division between the Holy Spirit and malevolent spirits.
All good things come from God. Therefore, evil or bad things are
from the adversary.

Faith is the key to positive expectation. The major negative spirits
are fear and doubt. These prevent people from accomplishing their
potential. Therefore, a positive attitude is from the Holy Spirit.
Likewise, a negative attitude is under the influence of evil spirits.

One of the positive instructions associated with the Spirit is to be
filled. Being filled simply means to be controlled.

...but be filled with the Spirit...

- Ephesians 5:18

On the other side of the coin, there are negative cautions. These concern negative actions that restrict the mental influence.

Quench not the Spirit.
- I Thessalonians 5:19

And grieve not the Holy Spirit of God...
- Ephesians 4:30

Therefore, it is a mental choice to be positively filled or to have a negative attitude. The negative restriction does not expel but it is an opposition to the Spirit. This is an action of going against the natural laws established by the Almighty. In some usages, this going against is called sin. By this deed, the person accepts the consequences when he violates the way the system was designed.

Control model ━━━━━━━━━━

The standard model for a control system illustrates the impact of a positive or negative mental, spirit state.

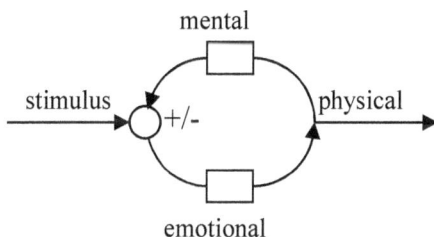

A stimulus causes an emotion to move forward. The emotion promotes a physical response. The mental process analyzes the response and feedback controls the emotion. The control may be positive reinforcement, which causes the physical response to grow. Or it may be a negative signal, which causes the physical reaction to deteriorate.

The emotion or will is the only element necessary during the birth of a response. As the system matures, the emotion has less influence. It is the mental feedback that multiplies growth by repetitive addition.

When a person is controlled by the spirit, he has a positive attitude or feedback. That causes positive growth. When a person grieves the spirit, he has a negative attitude or feedback that causes destruction.

As we have seen, a person has a choice under the natural laws governing human behavior. He can choose to make the positive decision, and have the rewards. Or he can choose to take the negative, and suffer the consequences. He is not forced into a decision. That freedom of choice is one of the greatest capacities given to mankind.

Change of control ━━━━━━━━━━━

There is a moment that a person concedes that Lord Jesus, the Christ is the ultimate guide, master, and teacher. It is in either this life or the next. In this life, the person is then under the influence of the Holy Spirit. This is referred to as receiving the Spirit. It does not necessarily mean being under the complete control of the intellect of God.

As that feedback from the Almighty becomes more positive, people grow and they become filled with the Spirit. The positive feedback implies there is a positive assent to God's control. If one rejects that influence, he quenches then grieves the Spirit. The relinquishing of influence to the Spirit of God is called conversion or change of control.

The influence of the Spirit is very personal. By observing the control model, we can reasonably expect the Spirit to impact our way of life.

> Don't you know that you yourselves are God's temple and that
> God's Spirit lives in you?
> - I Corinthians 3:16 NIV

The Spirit himself testifies with our spirit that we are God's children.
- Romans 8:16 NIV

Change point ──────

What is the effect of the Spirit at a person's change point in understanding *Who is this God?* That relationship brings us to the knowledge of truth about the Deity. A person must accept the reality of the intellectual Spirit to understand God.

Jesus answered, I tell you the truth, no one can enter the kingdom of God unless he is born of water and the Spirit.
- John 3:5 NIV

For we were all baptized by one Spirit into one body - whether Jews or Greeks, slave or free - and we were all given the one Spirit to drink.
- I Corinthians 12:13 NIV

Born of water and spirit is a simple statement about two of the trinity. It means born in a physical sense and in a positive mental sense.

The word baptism has caused much consternation among students of theology. It is a transliteration of the Greek word *baptizo (907)*. The early English translators did not have a similar concept, so they brought over the word intact.

Dr. Strong gave various shades of meaning to the original word translated as baptism: (1) to dip repeatedly, to immerse, to submerge (of vessels sunk), (2) to cleanse by dipping or submerging, to wash, to make clean with water, to wash one's self, bathe, (3) to overwhelm.

These two verses simply state a person must decide to come under the positive influence of the Spirit. That is the act of being baptized or converted to God's way of thinking.

Good old days ━━━━━━━━━

During the history of the Old Covenant, there were very few instances of spirit predominance. The Spirit of God came for a particular instance, and then departed from the person. It may return again, or it may depart permanently.

> And I will put my spirit within you, and cause you to walk in my statutes…
> - Ezekiel 36:27

We see an illustration of the temporary nature specifically in Samson, in Judges 13 and following. The Spirit came upon him several times.

We also see several occurrences of the Spirit coming on Saul in I Samuel 10 and following. In I Samuel 16:14, the Spirit departed and an evil spirit came.

This is very different from the New Dispensation.

> Up to that time the Spirit had not been given, since Jesus had not yet been glorified.
> - John 7:39

Now when a person accepts the Spirit influence, it is permanent. The statement succinctly declares the Spirit was not a gift prior to Jesus' departure. In earlier times, the Spirit was an occasional guest but not a permanent endowment.

The following declarations clarify that the good gift comes from the Father. Moreover, once a gift is given there is no change.

> If you had known me, you should have known my Father also: and from henceforth you know him, and have seen him.
> - John 14:7

> Every good gift and every perfect gift is from above, and comes down from the Father of lights, with whom is no variableness, neither shadow of turning.

- James 1:17

Ask and receive ───────────────

The old English word pray simply means ask. Pray is still used in our judicial system in the context of asking. Unfortunately, in common usage, this is another word that has become religious.

How do we talk to God? We cannot see with our natural senses. Vertical communications is by mental ascent of the Spirit.

> In the same way, the Spirit helps us in our weakness. We do not know what we ought to pray for, but the Spirit himself intercedes for us with groans that words cannot express.
> - Romans 8:26 NIV

We have observed that the Spirit of God is all around us. We called it a protector. We have also discussed that our intellect sets the ambiance or atmosphere around us.

Our communication comes through mental action. The more we release our physical and emotional, the greater our mental influence. The mental process permits comprehension in talking or praying. The transaction can be across the boundary from the physical world to the realm of the spirit world.

Review ───────────────

Address the following concepts.

1. The Spirit fits into which member of God?
2. What is the source of a positive attitude?
3. What is the source of negativity?
4. What is one word that describes the Spirit activity?
5. What is another word for spirit filled?
6. What is the meaning of baptize?

15

ANGELS - SPIRITS OF ANOTHER KIND

Thought
People are where they are
because of choices they make.
MOD

Variety of life ━━━━━━━━━

Our comprehension of the spiritual reality of the universe requires knowledge of other forces. This facet includes the complete creative acts for our world.

In earlier chapters, we found that God is a trinity. Mankind is in his likeness and has three perspectives of physical, emotional, and mental. In older English, these were called body, soul, and spirit. Similarly, the ultimate trinity is realized as Jesus the man, God the Almighty, and the Holy Spirit.

Now we will further investigate the creative act. During the process, we found that space or heavens *(shamayim, 8064)* and earth *(erets, 776)* were created. On the earth, there is a variety of life *(chay, 2416)*. The visible forms are plant life *(siyach, 7880)*, animal life *(nephesh, 5315)*, and human life. Only the later is in communication with the Creator God.

In a number of other locations, there is ample evidence that other beings were created. These beings are not physical as humans. They are called spirits or angels.

> Who makes his angels spirits; his ministers a flaming fire:
> - Psalm 104:4

Angel means exactly the same in Hebrew *(malak, 4397)* and Greek *(aggelos, 32)*. It is the very ordinary word for messenger or minister. The Hebrew term is used 214 times while the Greek is used 186 times in the Anthology. The word spirit is often used interchangeably with angel. The Hebrew word spirit *(ruwach, 7307)* occurs 378 times while the Greek spirit *(pneuma, 4151)* appears 385 times.

Realms

Where is the location of these nonphysical beings? A realm is the sphere or domain where someone resides. We propose to break the universe into three realms - natural, supernatural, and ultranatural.

The natural realm is the domicile of physical humans. The supernatural realm is the abode of the spirit arena. The ultranatural realm is the place of the Creator, God of the universe.

The critical thing to realize is all the realms exist in and overlay the same space. However there is a barrier between the realms that is one-directional. Beings in a lower realm cannot move up. They are restricted in their sphere of influence. However, higher realm occupants can move down.

By this understanding, mankind cannot have contact with the higher realms using the natural senses. However, the residents of the supernatural realm can be involved with things of the natural. This premise keeps an untouchable arena for the Creator that no spirit or physical being can penetrate. However, since God is a Spirit, he does have a place in the supernatural.

Angel created ━━━━━━━━━━━━━━

There is not an explicit statement that angels were created to be like anything else. However, there are very clear statements that they were formed as part of Creation.

> Praise the LORD. Praise the LORD from the heavens, praise him in the heights above.
> Praise him, all his angels, praise him, all his heavenly hosts.
> Praise him, sun and moon, praise him, all you shining stars.
> Praise him, you highest heavens and you waters above the skies.
> Let them praise the name of the LORD, for he commanded and they were created.
> He set them in place forever and ever; he gave a decree that will never pass away.
> - Psalm 148:1-6 NIV

> For by him all things were created: things in heaven and on earth, visible and invisible, whether thrones or powers or rulers or authorities; all things were created by him and for him.
> - Colossians 1:16 NIV

> Your settings and mountings were made of gold; on the day you were created they were prepared. You were anointed as a guardian cherub...
> - Ezekiel 28:13-14

The first description is about everything above the earth. The second description is about visible and invisible. The third seems to indicate that angels were created for a particular purpose.

There is a major difference between mankind and angels. The angels were all created in a mature, adult state. They do not procreate, age, or die, so the number stays constant.

Order in the court ━━━━━━━━━━━━━━

There is obviously a variety of angels. These have different power, intelligence, and abilities.

The medieval theologians had nine categories; Dr. Billy Graham had ten. The traditional hierarchy of angels is ranked from lowest to highest into the following orders: angels, archangels, principalities, powers, virtues, dominions, thrones, cherubim, and seraphim. Dr. Graham changed the middle five to the six principalities, authorities, powers, thrones, might, and dominion. Other writers combine the middle group to rulers and powers with the powers being the army for the rulers.

From our analysis, these could be restructured reasonably. Since the order is not specifically spelled out in one place, the categories are somewhat conjecture. By no stretch of the imagination, do we presume to have a unique insight. However, with present research, there seems to be an alternative match.

The hosts fit into three branches – personal, relations, and service. These functions have the same triad relationships that we have observed throughout the Holy Writ. Personal is an internal characteristic involving only one individual. Relations are an external or horizontal quality that engages multiple people. Deity service is the vertical feature that entails interaction with Almighty Yehovah.

Each of the branches has chiefs with the majority as troops. Archangels and angels are in the personal system that interacts with human spirits. Rulers and powers comprise the relations component. Cherubim and seraphim are in service to God.

The rank within each branch would not necessarily translate to another division. For example, a military general has little influence in a judge's civilian court.

Relations branch

In the relations branch, there are numerous different organizations with different criteria for power.

> For I am persuaded, that neither death, nor life, nor angels, nor principalities, nor powers, nor things present, nor things to come, nor height, nor depth, nor any other creature, shall be able to separate us from the love of God...
> - Romans 8:38

Other occasions identify additional indications of rank. An angel or spirit appears to be associated with every relations position of leadership and influence. There are angels for coaches, supervisors, and every political position.

This listing is simply to identify that the whole earth has order and structure. It also illustrates that everything we humans do is tied back to angelic or spirit influence.

Daniel, a prime minister under four kings, records one dramatic example. It illustrates that angels are intricately involved in government affairs. It also shows the power that is exercised when we request help from God.

> Daniel, since the first day that you set your mind to gain understanding and to humble yourself before your God, your words were heard, and I have come in response to them. But the prince of the Persian kingdom resisted me twenty-one days. Then Michael, one of the chief princes, came to help me, because I was detained there with the king of Persia. Now I have come to explain to you what will happen...
> - Daniel 10:12-14 NIV

Prince is a euphemism for the angel over a particular region. From Daniel's encounter, we find there are both helpful and restrictive princes. Notice that Michael is one of the chief princes. Obviously there are other chiefs in the host of angels.

Service branch ———————

In the service branch, there are only two organizations. Seraphim were winged creatures above the throne. They are explicitly mentioned only two times, and that in the same instance.

> I saw also the Lord sitting upon a throne, high and lifted up, and his
> train filled the temple. Above it stood the seraphims: each one had
> six wings; with twain he covered his face, and with twain he
> covered his feet, and with twain he did fly.
> - Isaiah 6:1

Cherubim were also winged beings but they are beside the thrown.
This appears to be the highest order or class. They have that special
association and power from having the confidence of the highest
official, God. These are similar to executive staff and guards. The
singular cherub is used on 30 occasions and the plural cherubim are
utilized in 65 instances. In current English the plural is often
cherubs.

Cherubim guarded the entrance to the Garden of Eden until the
deluge destroyed the site.

> So he drove out the man; and he placed at the east of the Garden of
> Eden Cherubim, and a flaming sword which turned every way, to
> keep the way of the tree of life.
> - Genesis 3:24

The golden figures guarding the mercy seat in the Holy of Holies
were cherubim. Unusual beings are described on other occasions.
Because of their features, they seem to fit in the deity service
classification. It is not very clear whether they are cherub or seraph.
However, the only incidence of seraphim is at the throne in the
account by Isaiah. Therefore, these other images are likely
cherubim.

An ancient prophet about 2500 years ago described a vision of
things to come in the future.

> And the living creatures ran and returned as the appearance of a
> flash of lightning.
> - Ezekiel 1:13

A later apostle in exile on the island of Patmos wrote a description
that also tends toward the cherubs.

...and round about the throne, were four beasts full of eyes before and behind.
- Revelation 4:6

Cherubs are not the little roly-poly guys with a bow and arrow. In folklore, the arrow caused a person to fall in love. In reality, cherubs are very powerful warriors with the authority of their commander, God Almighty.

Personal branch

In the personal branch that interacts with humans, there are only two titles, angel and archangel. Most of the spirits tend to fit into this multitude. The word angel is used 201 times and the plural is employed 94 times. In fact, the group is often called the host.

> But even the archangel Michael, when he was disputing with the devil about the body of Moses, did not dare to bring a slanderous accusation against him, but said, The Lord rebuke you!
> - Jude 9 NIV

The next way to identify angels is by names of what they do. Numerous picturesque identities are applied to these most unusual creatures. Some of these are ministering spirits, watchers, sons of God, chariots of God, holy ones, and miracles.

Other designations are associated with astronomical bodies. These names are heavenly bodies and morning stars.

Named ones

All the angelic beings apparently have names. However, in the traditional text, only three are specifically stated, Michael, Gabriel, and Lucifer.

Michael is the highest rank angel in the army. He is regaled five times in the chronicles. Archangel simply is chief angel. That places him as the commander in chief of the host. As such, he is intimately associated with any conflicts against adversary angels.

Gabriel means God's hero or the mighty one. He has the exalted position of being the one to bring the Most High's proclamations to mankind. He is noted four times and it is always bearing good news.

The third is Lucifer, which appears to refer to a guardian cherub. This would have placed him in the very presence with the ear and confidence of the Almighty. It appears that he was similar to a Chief of Staff. This position effectively has the power of his boss.

The guardian was created to have the highest authority in the cherub organization. However, his pride and desire for power led him to revolt. At that point, he lost the rights to his name.

Deuterocanonical ━━━━━━━━━━━━━

In some circles, another angel has a name. Raphael, the angel of healing, is a named messenger in the Deuterocanonical book of Tobit. This transcript declares there are seven angels who come before the Holy One.

> I am Raphael, one of the seven holy angels, which present the prayers of the saints, and which go in and out before the glory of the Holy One.
> - Tobit 12:15

Tobit is part of the Apocrypha. The Apocrypha are additions or appendices to the Old Testament. The manuscripts were a part of the Latin *Vulgate* and the Greek *Septuagint*. However, they were not in the Hebrew Bible, although written in that language. Two English translations of the supplemental books are available, the Authorized Version and the Revised Standard Version.

The Apocrypha was a common part of the King James Version when first translated in 1611 AD. In 1901 AD, a new translation, the American Standard Version, did not include the extra books. In time, many publishers of the Authorized Version dropped the records. The Apocrypha has been deleted from most other printings of the Bible as well.

The Greek and Russian Orthodox and Roman Catholic churches generally recognize the works. Many other groups only have a vague idea of the supplemental canon. There is no reference back to these writings from the New Testament authors. Therefore, many theologians do not depend on the works for theological basis.

Timing ———————

When were the angels created? It was necessarily during the creation process. Obviously, it was before the earth was developed. There is a clear inclination in the discourse between God with Job.

> Where were you when I laid the earth's foundation? ...while the morning stars sang together and all the angels shouted for joy?
> - Job 38:4-7

It appears the angels came into existence on the first or second day of creation. The significant events of the first three days of creation are progressively identified.

> And God said, Let there be light: and there was light.
> - Genesis 1:3

> And God called the firmament Heaven.
> - Genesis 1:8

> And God called the dry land Earth;
> - Genesis 1:10

The light in these references was before there were light sources. Moreover, angels are often associated with the heavens and lights of space. One name used was morning stars.

On the third day, earth was developed. The angels were already around to observe the foundations of earth and later mankind. At the conclusion of creation, a specific statement declares the host was formed during this time.

> Thus the heavens and the earth were finished, and all the host of them.
> - Genesis 2:1

On the sixth day at the completion of creation, everything was very good.

> And God saw every thing that he had made, and, behold, it was very good.
> - Genesis 1:31

Therefore, all the angels were necessarily good. However, things changed.

The angels observed the earth and mankind. Some of them wanted to move from their state to earth. Because of their supernatural powers they would be as gods to man. In addition, they would be able to partake of earth's beauty and pleasures.

This revolt came between the seventh day of creation and the dispute in the Garden of Eden. There the serpent directly challenged God's credibility.

> And the serpent said unto the woman, You shall not surely die: For God does know that in the day you eat thereof, then your eyes shall be opened, and you shall be as gods, knowing good and evil.
> - Genesis 3:4

The most intelligent but naïve humans believed the story. It seems they also wanted to be like gods and know evil as well as good.

Procreation ─────────────

The number of angels is extremely large. In multiple accounts, the description is an innumerable host. A fascinating point is that there are no indications of the number ever changing.

Since the count of angels is fixed, there is a necessary condition. There is no procreation between angels.

> When the dead rise, they will neither marry nor be given in marriage; they will be like the angels in heaven.
> - Mark 12:25 NIV

In the supernatural realm, there is no sexual ability to give birth. However, that does not mean the angels are without sexuality. Like the given names of the angels, every pronoun used is the masculine gender.

The ancient prophet Zechariah records one possible exception to the male rule. However, it is not clear that the women here are angels or just human representatives.

> Then lifted I up mine eyes, and looked, and, behold, there came out two women, and the wind was in their wings; for they had wings like the wings of a stork:
> - Zechariah 5:9

Perhaps the oldest document in the entire Biblical collection is by the ancient wise man, Job. Because of the structure and topics, it appears to have been written before any other testimony. The essay is a dialog between Job with God and Job with some friends. The first phase of the essay states the sons of God came with Satan. In the context it is apparent that the sons of God refers to angels.

> Now there was a day when the sons of God came to present themselves before the LORD *(Yehovah)*, and Satan came also among them.
> - Job 1:6

If we concede that another name of angels is sons of God, we find a very interesting story. This comes from the Genesis treatise in the collection of Scripture.

> The Nephilim *(5303)* were on the earth in those days, and also afterward, when the sons of God went to the daughters of men and had children by them. They were the heroes of old, men of renown.
> - Genesis 6:4 NIV

The complete narrative indicates that these super humans dropped to the human realm. Here they took to beautiful women. The resulting offspring were demigods, beings with human mothers and supernatural fathers.

The Nephilim *(5303)* is a name for giants. The word derivative means fallen one. They were called heroes; another term is Titans. The entire concept of supermen can be traced to this account. It appears much of Greek, Roman, and Norse mythology was derived from this report.

The time frame of the verse is just prior to the deluge of Noah. It was the conflict over these unnatural beings that brought on the flood and the resulting destruction of the contaminated race of humans.

Note the reference also alludes to another event afterwards. The second time the word Nephilim is used is to describe the sons of Anak. These awesome giants opposed the 12-man reconnaissance team of Moses as they were preparing to retake the ancient homeland.

> We saw the Nephilim there (the descendants of Anak come from the Nephilim). We seemed like grasshoppers in our own eyes, and we looked the same to them.
> - Numbers 13:33 NIV

Left home ━━━━━━━━━━━━

The intriguing idea is how did the spirit world beings take human functionality. A group of angels decided to leave their first supernatural realm and domicile on earth.

> And the angels, which kept not their first estate, but left their own habitation *(oiketerion, 3613)*, he has reserved in everlasting chains under darkness unto the judgment of the great day.
> - Jude 6

This was the rebellion in heaven or the spirit realm. Some of the angels saw the earth and the first people. They were proud of who they were and wanted at least two things from the earth. They were actually desirous of some of the abilities of people. This is even though in the supernatural realm they had an awesome state.

> For you have made him but little lower than God *(Elohiym, 430)*, and crowned him with glory and honor. You made him to have dominion over the works of your hands; you have put all things under his feet:
> - Psalm 8:5-6 ASV

Regardless of their remarkable status, they wanted more. In the supernatural realm they had a spirit abode *(oiketerion, 3613)*. Without a physical body, they could not experience many things. In that region, they could not participate in sexual activity. However, when they saw the beautiful earth women, they opted to take them on. Furthermore, by also having the supernatural realm power, they would appear to the mortals as gods.

I will

Lucifer made the declaration of desire for super power as he was proclaiming his 'I will'. The Prophet Isaiah records this in a most fascinating way.

> How are you fallen from heaven, O Lucifer, son of the morning! How are you cut down to the ground, which did weaken the nations!
>
> For you have said in your heart, I will ascend into heaven, I will exalt my throne above the stars of God: I will sit also upon the mount of the congregation, in the sides of the north: I will ascend above the heights of the clouds; I will be like the most High.
>
> Yet you shall be brought down to hell, to the sides of the pit.
> - Isaiah 14:12-15

The name Lucifer *(heylel, 1966)* means the morning star or shining one. It is used only one time in reference to the King of Babylon. Most theologians assert this statement refers to the fall of Satan.

In addition to the obvious context, there is precedent for this assertion. Daniel records an event regarding the prince of Persia. This also refers to Michael as a prince. It is apparent this is a euphemism for angels.

> But the prince of the kingdom of Persia withstood me one and twenty days: but, lo, Michael, one of the chief princes, came to help me; and I remained there with the kings of Persia.
> - Daniel 10:13

There are several intriguing ideas observed in the declaration recorded by Isaiah. It states 'I will' five times. The arrogance seems to challenge all other authority in the universe. Contrary to popular opinion, it does not appear that he plans to become God. It says be like the most High. That he desires to set up his own throne, there is no doubt, regardless of power of the Almighty.

He does say he will exalt his power over the stars of God, another name for angels. He also asserts he will sit upon the mount of the congregation in the sides of the north. This term is used in one other place where it appears to refer to the temple.

> Beautiful for situation, the joy of the whole earth, is mount Zion, on the sides of the north, the city of the great King.
> - Psalm 48:2

The revolting angels chose to descend to earth as part of their realm. A conflict ensued and they were removed from power in the loyal army of angels. Michael the archangel led the legion that overthrew the adversary and expelled him to earth.

> And there was war in heaven: Michael and his angels fought against the dragon; and the dragon fought and his angels, and prevailed not; neither was their place found any more in heaven.

> And the great dragon was cast out, that old serpent, called the Devil, and Satan, which deceives the whole world: he was cast out into the earth, and his angels were cast out with him.
> - Revelation 12:7-9

Center of the earth

Since this was a revolt, there was not provision for restoration. The war continues on earth. It will eventually be won. The final residence for the losers will be a place commonly called hell in English.

The Hebrew term *(sheol, 7585)* is used 65 times in the Old Testimony. Sheol is variously called the underworld, grave, hell, or pit.

The Greek term *(gehenna, 1067)* is used 12 times in the New Record. This was the valley of Hinnom, below Jerusalem. It was the garbage pit where filth and dead animals were burned in a continuous fire.

Another Greek term *(hades, 86)* is used 11 times as the equivalent of sheol. Hades was another name for Pluto the god of the lower regions. The location is also associated with Orcus or the nether world. That is a dark and dismal place in the very depths of the earth. The site is the common abode of disembodied spirits and the wicked. A similar place exists in the religion and mythology of virtually every culture.

Since creation was completed before the revolt, it appears this location was part of creation. But why would such a place exist in a perfectly created world? The description matches our present scientific understanding of the makeup of the earth's core. A super hot, molten environment is evidenced in volcanoes. The location of the source is at the center of the earth. The surface of the earth is covered with a thin crust only a few miles thick.

And the devil that deceived them was cast into the lake of fire and brimstone, where the beast and the false prophet are, and shall be tormented day and night forever and ever.
- Revelation 20:10

Then shall he say also unto them on the left hand, Depart from me, you cursed, into everlasting fire, prepared for the devil and his angels:
- Matthew 25:41

When the revolting angels took the earth estate, they were bound to it. The final conflict will simply remove them from the surface to the depths.

Light versus darkness ─────────────

The guardian cherub was a very influential angel. He was the most intelligent and beautiful creature in the realm. One of his dominions was the king of Tyre. This is very similar to the earlier discussion about the king of Babylon and the prince of Persia.

Son of man, take up a lament concerning the king of Tyre and say to him: This is what the Sovereign LORD says:

You were the model of perfection, full of wisdom and perfect in beauty. You were in Eden, the garden of God; every precious stone adorned you: ruby, topaz and emerald, chrysolite, onyx and jasper, sapphire, turquoise and beryl. Your settings and mountings were made of gold; on the day you were created, they were prepared.

You were anointed as a guardian cherub, for so I ordained you. You were on the holy mount of God; you walked among the fiery stones. You were blameless in your ways from the day you were created till wickedness was found in you.

Through your widespread trade you were filled with violence, and you sinned. So I drove you in disgrace from the mount of God, and I expelled you, O guardian cherub,
- Ezekiel 28:12-18

The only known participants in Eden were Adam, Eve, God, and the malevolent serpent. Since this entity was in Eden, this obviously is not the physical king of Tyre, but the one that controlled him.

The discourse clearly declares that he was created perfect. After he revolted at Eden, his name was changed. The Hebrew term *Satan (7854)* means adversary. The Greek word *diablos (1228)* means slanderer and is translated into English as devil. Another Greek word *daimon (1142)* is the basis for the English demon and is translated devils.

Beelzebub *(954)*, the prince of the devils, is from the Aramaic meaning lord of the flies (fliers). Abaddon *(3)* was the Hebrew angel of the bottomless pit in Revelation 9:11. In Greek that name was Apollyon *(3)*.

The angel of light became the power of darkness.

> Who hath delivered us from the power of darkness, and hath translated us into the kingdom of his dear Son:
> - Colossians 1:13

Because the angels were rebels from their first realm, they were bound to the one of their choice. This is just like humans. When we make an event with others, we can never go back and undo it.

> And the angels, which kept not their first estate, but left their own habitation, he hath reserved in everlasting chains under darkness unto the judgment of the great day.
> - Jude 6

Chains under darkness indicates they do not have light. Everlasting indicates they do not have a chance to change their ways and return. This is very unlike humans, who can change their allegiance and receive forgiveness.

At the time of the angelic revolt, light was associated with Lucifer. However, in all other instances it is very explicitly identified with the Creator.

In him was life; and the life was the light of men. And the light
shines in the darkness; and the darkness has not understood it.
- John 1:4-5 NIV

How big was the revolt? About one-third of the angels preferred the
earth idea to be gods.

And his tail drew the third part of the stars of heaven, and did cast
them to the earth: and the dragon stood...
- Revelation 12:4

When the insurgent angels moved to the earth, their name was
changed also. They became known as devils, which is obviously a
play on words for the evil.

Super majority ─────────────

One comment is appropriate. Although one-third of the angels
became demon spirits, two-thirds remained loyal and in the service
of the Almighty. The guys in the white hats are twice as numerous.

There are ample examples where Michael, the loyal leader, has
more power than the adversary. Majority number, command of
Michael, and total power of Yehovah, assures the outcome of any
conflict. Logically, it makes sense to side with the good guys. They
will ultimately win any challenge.

Review ─────────────

Address the following concepts.

1. What are the three branches of angels?
2. What is the difference in an angel and a spirit?
3. What is another name for malevolent spirits?
4. Who were the angels that were given a name?
5. How does a spirit come into the human system?
6. Where is the spirit realm in relationship to the physical world?
7. What is the Apocrypha or Deuterocanonical books?

16

OTHER GODS

The tale tells ━━━━━━━━━━━━━

Any item or concept that has great value and merit will have copies attempted. These knock-offs are not real, but imitations. That is also true in the relationship with the Creator of the universe. There is a long history of challenges between the God of heaven and the usurper.

Much of the anthology about the God of the universe deals about conflict with adversaries. Therefore, it is appropriate for a study of theology to address these false gods.

We will use the Babylonian and Greek gods as an illustration. There are similar stories and structures in virtually every culture. These tales in many ways have likeness to the Holy Writ. The pattern typically falls into a familiar structure.

There is a supreme god, but he is not usually the creator. Multiple other deities are associated with nature or parts of life. The gods are usually promiscuous and particularly find mortal women attractive. A responsibility of the super beings is to provide for humans. A celestial region is reserved for the divinities. Mortals reside on the earth. A hostile place below the earth is reserved for enemies and serious lawbreakers.

One thing is missing. There is no redeemer to salvage the mortals into a perfect afterlife. By distorting the reality of the oldest, commonly used record, focus is placed on false deities. This keeps the worshippers in bondage to the fiends.

The story of the other gods is oppressive. Unfortunately, many Christians have made the Creator harsh and oppressive. That is not the case when the Spirit is the controlling influence in your life. The Judeo-Christian view of God is the only version that promotes joy, peace, and success.

Early time ─────────

The first challenge came before the Garden of Eden, in the halls of the ancients. The Creator had made a group of beings variously called angels or spirits. Since one third of the Trinity is the Spirit, it is reasonable to expect entities in the spirit realm.

These were introduced in the previous chapter. One-third of the angels revolted to set-up an adversarial kingdom where they could be gods on earth. The other two-thirds remained as loyal envoys of the Almighty.

This chapter will address two different aspects of the evil empire. First, there are angels who became demons. Because of their super natural power they actually appear as gods to human beings.

The second group of players is men who let the malevolent spirits control their thought process. The most visible of these angels were from the relations branch. By this process, the men have the power and influence of the fiends. Their extra natural influence installs some of these men as apparent gods.

Men and women of great power and influence are often elevated to hero worship. This even happens with sports figures, music stars, actors, and politicians. The next step is godlike adoration. The transition to godhood is particularly easy in societies with oral or even limited written traditions.

What manner of person is this ⸻

The sons of God saw the daughters of men. Who were the sons of God? Several possibilities can be argued. In the last chapter, we found they are the angels.

Some versions of the *Septuagint* contain the word angels for sons of God. This ancient Greek translation provides a good correlation to use with our English versions.

> There were giants in the earth in those days; and also after that, when the sons of God came in unto the daughters of men, and they bare children to them, the same became mighty men which were of old, men of renown.
> - Genesis 6:4

There were giants in the earth. Consider next the word that is translated giant. This is the Hebrew word *nephilim (5303)*. The *Septuagint* also translates this word as giants.

Nevertheless, some scholars prefer to consider these as fierce warriors or heroes. There is considerable basis for this. The end of the verse refers to them as mighty and men of renown. In addition, hero is a concept applied to some of the gods of mythology. However, the root of the word *nephilim* commonly means fallen one.

Our culture tends to dismiss angels and spirits as things from another era or residing in another world. The argument goes, no one has seen an angel or can prove they exist, so they are probably not real. Many things invisible do exist and have profound influence.

If there is a God, there are obviously spirits or angels of some sort that reside in his service realm. Although God is not seen with the senses, there is substantial evidence for extraordinarily strong power and influence. It is appropriate to refer to this inexplicable being by the commonly recognizable name of God.

The idea of giants is not unique. The concept of supernatural men marrying beautiful mortal women was common in ancient mythology. The demigods resulting from the union carried both the power of the gods and the body of humans.

However, the intermarriage resulted in a corruption of both lineages. The resulting offspring were mutants. Regardless of the heritage of the men, they were evil and developed a very evil society.

Greek and Roman titans closely parallel the description presented. Since mythology is usually based in some historical fact, it seems the scripture account has further secular correlation.

Some would argue that the Genesis account derives from the mythology of the time. The better-documented indications are that mythology was based on the same events.

The Genesis account was recorded by the court-trained historian, Moses. History by necessity is written after the fact based on the best evidence available. Mythology tended to be a more oral tradition and as such, it was easily modified with each telling.

Nimrod ────────────

One of the first individuals that became a god was Nimrod. Nimrod, who was emperor of Babel in Chaldea, was also called Ninus, founder of Ninevah in Assyria.

> Cush was the father of Nimrod, who grew to be a mighty warrior on the earth. He was a mighty hunter before the LORD; that is why it is said, Like Nimrod, a mighty hunter before the LORD. The first centers of his kingdom were Babylon, Erech, Akkad and Calneh, in Shinar. From that land he went to Assyria, where he built Nineveh, Rehoboth Ir, Calah and Resen, which is between Nineveh and Calah; that is the great city.
> - Genesis 10:8-12 NIV

Nimrod instilled emperor worship. He took the dragon as his personal emblem. With his passing, the priests of his religion deified him as the god Marduk. Is it not interesting that a mortal man was knowingly made a god by his constituents?

Marduk's deity was represented in as many as 50 different god names. The deity was called Bel in Babylon, Baal in Canaan, and Cronus in Greek.

Notice the etymology of the word between the god's name Bel and the name of the city Ba'bel. He was also the god of fertility and sexual expression. His worship often involved licentious acts. Other manifestations included the tradition as Melkarth/Hercules.

In extrabiblical accounts, his wife was Semiramis, the great mysterious queen of Assyria. When deified she was called Astarte or Ishtar, the queen of heaven.

Semiramis had a son Tammuz. The religious cult of a mother and son became Isis and Osiris of Egypt. The Greeks called them Venus and Adonis. The Latin culture brings them to this day as the queen of heaven and son.

Egypt

Many of the ancient Egyptian religious practices have parallels in the Babylonian religions. The Egyptian worship customs have been attributed to Nimrod's grandmother, who was the wife of Ham.

By a few sources, she was called Zeptah or Egyptus. In ancient language structure, Egyptus is an unusual spelling for a female person. The eldest son of Ham and Zeptah was Pharaoh, who established the first government in the Nile country.

Both Egyptian and Babylonian religions have a common basis. But they evolved somewhat differently in the east and west Hamitic practices. Some of the rituals continue into modern lore and sects.

It is unnecessary to use secular events to verify the Scriptural accounts. However, critics often try to discredit the religious record as unscientific or myths. When archaeology and other recorded history have related accounts, it can be used as correlation.

Online encyclopedia ━━━━━━━━━

One tremendous source for information is obviously the Internet. However, a researcher must be careful with this information. Since it is not peer reviewed, anyone can stick garbage out there with his opinion. Nevertheless, it still can be a phenomenal resource, if used with caution.

Perhaps one of the biggest assets in mythology is an internet encyclopedia. Notice the huge number of different gods addressed by this reference. "This is an encyclopedia on mythology, folklore, legends, and more. It contains over 5700 definitions of gods and goddesses, supernatural beings and legendary creatures and monsters from all over the world. This is by no means a complete work…"

Most casual students knew there were ancient Greek and Roman gods from school literature. Some are also aware that the days of the week are named for Norse gods. Past that, in our culture, we tend to ignore the other gods. With over 5700 identified ones, there is obviously a tremendous influence on every society.

The Greek titans ━━━━━━━━━

Greek mythology is the most developed that has influence in the Western culture. The first of the gods was Chaos, the great void or primordial lump within the universe. Chaos can refer to the creation, the flood, Ham, or Noah. A great-grandson of Chaos correlates to Nimrod, who was a grandson of Ham. Therefore, it is likely Chaos refers to the flood era principals.

Chaos had three offspring without a mate. These were Eros (sexual desire), Gaia (mother earth), and Tarturus (the lowest region of the world). Tarturus is below Hades, the place for the dead. The foundation of the Greek legends is Gaia, mother earth. Everything that was came from her. Without a mate, she gave birth to her first-born Uranus (sky), Ourea (mountains) and Pontus (sea).

Her son Uranus became her husband and fathered many races. The most notable ethnic group was the godlike giants called titans. The titans were six sons and six daughters of Uranus and Gaia. The twelve titans were the embodiment of the forces of nature. Each son married one of his sisters.

The youngest titan, Cronus (harvest), with Rhea (mother of gods) birthed the six Olympian gods. Cronus is the Greek name for the Babylonian god that was King Nimrod.

The Olympians included three goddesses and three gods. Demeter was goddess of earth and fertility, while Hera was queen goddess of marriage and birth. Hestia was the virgin goddess of the hearth fire. Hades, Poseidon and Zeus became the rulers of the Olympian universe.

The next titan, Iapetus (Japeth), and Themis (justice) produced Atlas, Menoetius, Prometheus and Epimetheus. Themis is the image of a blindfolded woman holding a pair of scales and a cornucopia. She has oracle powers and by her nephew Zeus, she is the mother of the Horae and the Moirae. This goddess is the symbol of the American legal system.

Two sets of titans were less notorious. Oceanus (ocean) and Tethys (fertile ocean) had over 3000 offspring such as rivers and springs. Hyperion (before the sun) and Theia procreated Helios (sun), Eos (dawn) and Selene (moon).

Another titan, Crius married Mnemosyne (memory). She became mother of the nine Muses by Zeus, her nephew.

The final titans, Coeus wed Phoebe who originally owned the oracle of Delphi. They were the parents of Asteria and Leto, the mother of Apollo and Artemis.

The other races from mother earth were equally notorious. Gaia gave birth to the Cyclops, the emotional giants with one round eye in their foreheads. She also birthed the three Hecatonchires, fierce giants with 100 arms and 50 heads. Other offspring were the Erinyes, the spirits of punishment.

At the request of Gaia (mother earth), Cronus castrated his father Uranus. The Gigantes (monstrous giants) were conceived when his potent blood fell to mother earth. Cronus cast the genitals over his shoulder into the sea. The resulting foam was the birthplace of Aphrodite and nymphs - spirits of nature.

The Greek Olympians ━━━━━━━━━━

Zeus led the revolt against his grandfather, Uranus, and the dynasty of his uncles, the titans. When he defeated the titans, he banished them to Tartarus, the lowest region in earth. Once Zeus had total control, he and his Olympian brothers divided the universe. Zeus gained the heavens, Poseidon the sea, and Hades the underworld.

Zeus was the supreme god of Mount Olympus and of the pantheon who lived there. As the supreme ruler, he was responsible for the law, justice and morals. Zeus was originally worshiped as a weather deity by the Greek tribes.

Zeus had to defend his heavenly kingdom from other uncles. Three separate assaults were from the offspring of Gaia, mother earth. They were the Gigantes, Typhon, and the twins Aloadae. Zeus fought them with his thunderbolt and aegis, a shield from the skin of the divine goat, Amaltheia. As with the titans, Zeus banished them all to Tartarus, below the underworld.

Although responsible for morals, Zeus was promiscuous. His consorts numbered well over one hundred. He fathered children by relatives, goddesses, nymphs (spirits of nature), and mortals. Legends claim the children of Zeus gave mankind all that was needed to live in an orderly, moral way.

Israel foreigners ━━━━━━━━━━

There are numerous outside gods identified in the Old Testament of the Book. You will notice there are numerous names for the same god. The designation changed with different cultures, languages, and attributes.

The most common was Baal *(Bamowth, 1120)*, a Phonecian phallic deity. His Babylonian-Sumerian name was Marduk, the god name of King Nimrod. The Hebrew rendition of Marduk was Merodach *(4781)*. Moloch *(4428)* or Molekh was the entirely malevolent rendition of Baal, to whom children were sacrificed.

Baal was called Ashur, as the patron god of Assyria. His wife was Ishtar. Baal's consort was also called Ashtoreth *(6253)*, Asherah, Anath, or Astarte, a Phoneician goddess of fertility and sex. She is equivalent to the Greek goddess Aphrodite.

Beelzebub *(954)* is the patron god of the Philistines in ancient Palestine. Beelzebub is the prince of evil spirits and the name means lord of the flies (fliers). In Milton's Paradise Lost, he is Satan's chief lieutenant.

Belial *(1100)* is the evil spirit of darkness and godlessness in old Palestine. Belial can also be compared with Satan.

Dagon *(1712)* is an ancient Mesopotamian vegetation god of the Philistines, and father of Baal. Dagon is one of the old gods but his temple at Ashdod existed right up until the time of Jesus. Dagon was portrayed half man and half fish. These characteristics make him appear to be associated with Ham who came out of the flood. Ham was the grandfather of Nimrod, a mortal who became Marduk or Baal.

Although it is not a god, there is a term from Jewish mythology that is important to know. Abracadabra is a cabalistic (pattern) charm that was supposed to get rid of any illness. It may be from the Hebrew *Ab* (Father), *ben* (Son), and *ruwach acadsch* (Holy Spirit).

Another possibility is that it is from the first few letters of the Phoenician alphabet (A-B ra-C a-D abra). It is related to the name of an old disease demon. The term is still used by modern-day conjurers.

What is next

The legends of most gods are very repressive, domineering, and demeaning. The Book view of God is the only story of a deity that universally promotes joy, peace, and success.

The following chapter returns to deal with the various spirits identified by the Scripture. These impact every facet of human existence. That insight will explain the unusual nature of some of the other gods in our culture. The discussion will also illustrate how mankind can react to the supernatural influences and win.

Review

Identify the following.

1. Who were the sons of God?
2. What is another designation for angels?
3. How did giants come about?
4. Where was the primary location of Nimrod's kingdom?
5. Who was Nimrod's wife?
6. Who did Baal or Bel represent?
7. Who was the founder of the Babylonian religion?
8. Who was founder of the Egyptian religion?
9. Who was her son?
10. Who was the Greek mother of the living?
11. How many Greek titans were there?
12. What is Tarturus?
13. Who was the chief Olympian god?
14. What is missing from mythology to salvage mortals?

17

ANGEL OF THE LORD

Thought
Bless the Lord, O my soul
And all that is within me.
Bless the Lord, O my soul
And forget not all his benefits.
Psalm 103:1 - 2

Another angel

In the study of the angelic realm, a unique messenger crops up. This one is called angel of the Lord. The generic concept, an angel of the LORD *(Yehovah)*, appears 9 times. The specific being, the angel of the LORD *(Yehovah)*, occurs 59 times. In thirteen other places, angel of God *(Elohiym)* is used. After the herald is introduced in a story, in later references he may be referred to simply as the angel. This construction indicates an explicit messenger.

Who is this special envoy? The first is a specific reference in a personal conversation with Abraham's mistress, Hagar.

> And the angel of the LORD found her by a fountain of water in the wilderness, by the fountain in the way to Shur. And he said, Hagar, Sarai's maid, whence came you?
> - Genesis 16:7-8

The first discussion by the angel of God was also with Abraham's maid. It is clear from these two examples, that the angel of the LORD and the angel of God is the same messenger in both conversations.

> And God heard the voice of the lad; and the angel of God called to Hagar out of heaven, and said unto her, What ails you, Hagar?
> - Genesis 21:17

The first generic identification is in an exchange with the nation Israel. The event occurs just after the passing of the great General Joshua.

> And an angel of the LORD came up from Gilgal to Bochim, and said, I made you to go up out of Egypt, and have brought you unto the land which I sware unto your fathers; and I said, I will never break my covenant with you.
> - Judges 2:1

The final occurrence is with the death of Herod, during the first part of the first century AD. It is interesting that this occurs during the Acts of the Apostles. There are no further references to angel of the Lord after the Acts throughout history.

> And immediately the angel of the Lord smote him, because he gave not God the glory: and he was eaten of worms, and gave up the ghost.
> - Acts 12:23

These examples provide the framework for analysis and discussion.

Could it be ⸻

The function of the angel of the Lord is personal contact with people. Since people reside in the natural realm, they cannot see up to the higher realms. All relationships involving the five senses must be on the physical level.

The relationship of personal human contact may have been originally delegated to another being. There are indications by some theologians that Lucifer may have originally been assigned to this office. When he revolted to become an earth god, that agency became vacant.

When human communication is necessary, the position must be fulfilled. Rather than have an agent perform the function, Yehovah himself took on the role. God is capable of all positions within the universe he created.

Hence, the physical person of the Creator was perceptible from time to time. When Yehovah came to earth as Jesus, he was responsible for personal interaction with humans. After he departed the earth, his Spirit returned as a permanent comforter and protector. Therefore, once the Spirit was fully active, there was no longer a need for the angel of Lord. This is logical since, as we saw earlier, spirit is another representation of an angel.

Contact ——————

In each illustration, it is obvious that the discussion is personally representing Yehovah. In many of these cases, the angel takes on human form.

Consensus is that angel of the Lord refers to the physical personification of the trinity. Hence, this would be the same member as the man Jesus. The appearance of God in physical form is called a theophany.

Consider an insightful question. When God is in human form, does he still have all the authority and power throughout the universe? Of course, he is still God!

Contrast this with the glory or essence of God, which was apparent on several occasions. No one can look on that and live to tell the tale. Moses encountered that emotional will just before he was given the Ten Commandments.

And he said, You cannot see my face: for there shall no man see
me, and live.
- Exodus 33:20

The Old Tribute occurred before the birth of the physical god-man.
Therefore, any physical realization must necessarily take on a
unique form. Since angels resided in the supernatural realm, they
could descend to the natural realm. So, by assuming the form of an
angel, it was possible for Yehovah to physically appear before the
birth of the God-man.

Other angels walk about the earth observing what is happening.
They report to the angel of Yehovah.

And they answered the angel of the LORD *(Yehovah)* that stood
among the myrtle trees, and said, We have walked to and fro
through the earth, and, behold, all the earth sits still, and is at rest.
- Zechariah 1:11

Guardians

Do you have a guardian angel? There is not one but many that are
charged with guarding a person. The primary function of these
particular agents is to protect the individual.

The angel of the LORD *(Yehovah)* encamps around those who fear
him, and he delivers them.
- Psalm 34:7

For he will command his angels concerning you to guard you in all
your ways...
- Psalm 91:11 NIV

Take heed that you despise not one of these little ones; for I say
unto you, That in heaven their angels do always behold the face of
my Father which is in heaven.
- Matthew 18:10

And he answered, fear not: for they that be with us are more than they that be with them. And Elisha prayed, and said, LORD *(Yehovah)*, I pray you, open his eyes, that he may see. And the LORD *(Yehovah)* opened the eyes of the young man; and he saw: and, behold, the mountain was full of horses and chariots of fire round about Elisha.
- II Kings 6:16-17

An interesting thought is who or what are the angels guarding against. In a now imperfect world, there are malevolent spirits or angels that are trying to control persons. The guardians perform the militia function of protection against these vices.

Spirit condition ━━━━━━━━━━━━━━

In their supernatural estate, angels do not reside in a physical body. They were created to communicate with people through the mental pathway. This route is sometimes called spirit, attitude, or atmosphere.

But to which of the angels said he at any time, Sit on my right hand, until I make your enemies your footstool? Are they not all ministering spirits, sent forth to minister for them who shall be heirs of salvation?
- Hebrews 1:13-14

There are numerous examples of an angel particularly influencing a human mental state. In some instances, the input is called a vision. In others, the inspiration is via a dream.

But after he had considered this, an angel of the Lord appeared to him in a dream...
- Matthew 1:20

Perhaps a more modern word that fits the spirits impact is called an attitude. In most cases, the influence is simply what is called a thought.

Review ───────────

Address the following concepts.

1. Who is the angel of the Lord?
2. What is the function of the angel of the Lord?
3. Are there angels that are assigned to you?
4. What is the function of these angels?

18

GIFTS OF SPIRIT

Thought
God will not do things for you,
but He will help you.

Talents ──────────

Numerous capabilities are described as gifts of the spirit. The dictionary describes gifts in this connotation as a notable capacity, talent, or endowment.

> There are different kinds of gifts, but the same Spirit.
> - I Corinthians 12:4 NIV

> And in the church God has appointed first of all apostles, second prophets, third teachers, then workers of miracles, also those having gifts of healing, those able to help others, those with gifts of administration, and those speaking in different kinds of tongues.
> - I Corinthians 12:28 NIV

The gifts of the spirit are separated into three types. These are searching, service, and sign abilities. The searching talents fit into the educational mental category of the model. The service aptitude is the physical group. The sign capabilities are in the emotional phase.

The searching abilities are apostles, prophets, and teachers. Similarly, the service skills are helpers, administrators, and most healing. The sign talents are miracles, tongues, and some healing.

Operation ────────────

As noted earlier, the emotional phase is part of the birthing or initiation process. Similarly, the mental process is the maturing or control component.

Hence, the sign gifts were a critical element during the formation of the Christian culture. They become less prominent as the community matures. Today, when translators go into a totally new, isolated culture, the sign talents may be very significant. Similarly, the ability may arise in developing new Christians. However, their importance diminishes as a person matures in faith and knowledge.

Initially, the physical body reacts to emotional stimulus. Any emotion can be trained by focusing on it. It is possible thus to exercise the sign gifts in environments other than to get the attention of unbelievers. However, the normal process of intellectual curiosity and development tends to override the emotional.

As recorded by the early intellectual Paul of Tarsus, the signs are illustrations for birthing new Christians. He continues that the searching or mental gifts are for maturing and growing. We are instructed to mature and seek the intellectual talents for personal development.

> Follow the way of love and eagerly desire spiritual gifts, especially the gift of prophecy.
> - I Corinthians 14:1 NIV

> He who speaks in a tongue edifies himself, but he who prophesies edifies the church.
> - I Corinthians 14:4 NIV

> Tongues, then, are a sign, not for believers but for unbelievers; prophecy, however, is for believers, not for unbelievers.

- I Corinthians 14:22 NIV

Exercise of the sign gifts is not an integral component to being a great person of faith. The good news by John the Apostle explicitly states John the Baptizer did no signs.

> ...and many people came to him. They said, though John never performed a miraculous sign, all that John said about this man was true.
> - John 10:41

In addition, none of the later letters by Paul or others gives record of exercising the sign abilities. However, in all instances, people are implored to grow in wisdom and knowledge.

Searching Group

The searching talents provide the educational process. They include apostles, prophets, and teachers. The first, an apostle, is one sent on a mission to initiate an important belief. Since there can only be a few initiators, this number is limited by definition. The apostles enter an arena first.

The second, prophecy, simply means insight or to proclaim. A more common related word in present vernacular is to preach or advocate. Proclaimers are the leaders that build on the work of the apostles.

Third, teachers have advanced knowledge and education, which gives them the ability to instruct or show others. Rather than being advocates, teachers tend to pass on information.

Miracle workers

One of the sign gifts was a worker of miracles. What are these wonders? Miracles are things that are not comprehended by current knowledge and understanding. We must be careful to identify what is common knowledge to one may be a miracle to another because of a different understanding of physical laws.

Who Is This God?

Miracles are not magic which is slight of hand, tricks, and cleverness that the audience does not see or comprehend. Great care must be exercised with magic, since this ability can also be associated with the nether world.

> But the cowardly, the unbelieving, the vile, the murderers, the sexually immoral, those who practice magic arts, the idolaters and all liars - their place will be in the fiery lake of burning sulfur. This is the second death.
> - Revelation 21:8 NIV

Seldom do we find someone who consistently is able to work miracles. That seems to be intriguing. Logically it would be expected that there would be approximately an equal number of miracles as other gifts.

Could it be that miracles are physical and can be touched and analyzed? Or is it simply a lack of faith or confidence in the Word?

> You didn't have enough faith, Jesus told them. I assure you, even if you had faith as small as a mustard seed you could say to this mountain, Move from here to there, and it would move. Nothing would be impossible.
> - Matthew 17:20 NIV

Who among us really believes and practices that the promise literally applies to moving dirt. Or is it a euphemism for moving obstacles in our life?

Every believer is given the power of miracles by speaking our faith. There are numerous other promises to develop our comprehension of the power that God has given us.

> Death and life are in the power of the tongue:
> - Proverbs 18:21
>
> I can do all things through Christ, which strengthens me.
> - Philippians 4:13
>
> If you shall ask any thing in my name, I will do it.

- John 14:14

...You do not have, because you do not ask God.
- James 4.2 NIV

It is very clear that we must verbalize our expectations and desires before the results happen.

Be well ━━━━━━━━━━━━━

Healing is one of the talents that have been subject to some confusion of concepts. It fits most often in the service category and occasionally in the sign arena. To clear the record, from our experience, we are great believers in personal healing through the Spirit. With that, let us look at healing from the analytical perspective of a scientist.

In every ancient culture, there was a medicine man or priest. His primary method of art was to invoke incantations. For certain conditions, he was the wizard who knew the magical abilities of plants. As medicine developed, we found it was not magic but chemical compounds in the herbs.

In fact, one of the words translated witchcraft in an early version was *pharmakeia (5331)*. The word derivatives are also translated as sorcery.

> Idolatry, witchcraft *(5331)*, hatred, ...that they, which do such things, shall not inherit the kingdom of God.
> - Galatians 5:20-21

> ..and whoremongers, and sorcerers *(5331)*, and idolaters, and all liars, shall have their part in the lake which burns with fire and brimstone: which is the second death.
> - Revelation 21:8

It is obvious that the word is similar to pharmacy, a place of compounding and distributing drugs. The translation (*pharmakeia, 5331)* falls into three different drug related categories. It can be using or administering drugs, poisoning, or sorcery and magical arts.

Is there any less faith involved on the part of the doctor and patient than with the medicine man? No! My grandmother learned about herbs from her grandmother. She had a special gift of healing because of that knowledge. However, my adult children search books and the Internet. They have more information than Grandmother ever dreamed. They can treat a much larger variety of things and have a greater expectancy of consistent success.

Moreover, with increased information available, we have found many things impact health. This includes diet, exercise, water and air quality, and sunlight. Now, a medicinal man is not always necessary. Our intellect directs us to use pain relievers, vitamins and herbs, or precautions for some conditions. Furthermore, we pray through the Spirit and seek wisdom on how to treat other ailments.

Incantations of the medicine man can work. They can cause psychosomatic or emotional impact on physical conditions. However, the medical arts are more logical analysis and physical repair. With learning, we are more dependent on the intellectual knowledge or spirit for healing.

The appearance of the talents has changed from the medicine man or priest to the medical man. Nevertheless, it is still a spirit or intellect ability based on information provided by the Creator.

Moreover, healing is involved with the expectation or belief it will work. Sometimes there is healing past just what we can intellectually understand. That has to be the Spirit of God and no one else.

Service Group

Service is the assistance of someone. This includes helps, administration, and healing in some cases. The talent of helps is aid, assistance, or support built on a personal relationship. This can be by giving time, finances, or technical advice. Everyone who contributes money to a project is exercising the gift of helps.

Administration is associated with organizations and government. Administration is the background service that no one sees. These tasks are often office positions that are critical to keep the machinery of the business operating.

Language ────────────────

Language as we have seen earlier is the method of communicating within a family group. Language is learned; therefore, it is intellectual or mental. A person can make a decision to learn a new language. Place a child in the environment, and he readily grasps multiple languages.

Language has structure and rules. In emotional situations, we revert to our mother tongue because of our comfort. Children raised in other cultures have a mother tongue separate from the parents.

This was quite common in the French speaking area of Louisiana where we were raised. A similar circumstance was observed with the Spanish speakers when we lived in Texas and California. The parents often maintain the old culture language. Nevertheless, the children readily adopt the ubiquitous English language of their surroundings. Often they reject and cannot speak the traditional language of the parents.

The scripture has discussions in the book of Acts and I Corinthians about speaking other languages. Two words are used for language. The word dialect is obtained from one of the terms *(dialektos, 1258)*. It is translated language one time and tongue five times in Acts, the book penned by the physician Dr. Luke.

The second word translated as language *(glossa, 1100)* is used fifty times throughout the New Record. In some cases it obviously refers to the member of the body in the mouth that makes speech. In other cases it is rendered as a particular or unique language.

It is the mouth organ in the books of Mark, Luke, Romans, Philippians, James, I Peter, and I John. The word is obviously language in Revelation. In Acts and I Corinthians 12 – 14, it is used both as the mouth organ and as a unique language. To illustrate the idea of a particular lingo, some translations use the modifier different, a, or unknown before the word language.

Among serious scholars, there are three interpretations of speaking in other languages or tongues. Some think the language is a foreign tongue that is spoken for the alien listeners. Another group contends the language is a special communications between true believers and the Spirit. Others argue it is a temporary language as a demonstration for new believers.

As with most things, the reality appears to be a combination. We noted above that the sign abilities were primarily for getting the attention of unbelievers. In addition, during the era of the writing, numerous languages were used in the city.

The local and religious language was Hebrew. The educational language was Greek. The language of the Roman government was Latin. The adjacent language from surrounding areas was Arabic. Pilgrims to the religious temple often were from foreign areas with another language. Therefore, a very important ability would be to communicate in some or all of these languages.

We experienced a similar condition recently when we visited India. The local language was Punjabi. There are 26 such states and each has at least one regional languages. The national and religious language was Hindi. The economic trade language was English. The Moslem and Pakistani culture used Arabic. School children are fluent in at least three languages, the local, national, and English.

Fortunately, we could conduct our business in English. Nevertheless, when our hosts spoke one of the other languages, it was an unknown tongue to us. The gift of languages is obviously a very valuable element of culture.

Outside the realm of known language, special communication has been demonstrated to happen on at least three planes. First, when we are in deep thought or a very close relationship, we can communicate with unusual sounds. Second, the practice has been observed in a variety of religious cultures. Third, I remember a discussion in a graduate university class about learning the technique to help development in creative acts of art and music. This creates an altered state of thought.

Free indeed

The Spirit gives one very substantial gift that is not registered in the traditional list. That is the gift of freedom. Man was not intended to be subservient or dominated by guilt, legalism, or oppressive attitudes. Humans are free when the positive spirit is the major influence on the person.

> Now the Lord is the Spirit, and where the Spirit of the Lord is, there is freedom.
> - II Corinthians 3:17 NIV

> ...because through Christ Jesus the law of the Spirit of life set me free from the law of sin and death.
> - Romans 8:2 NIV

> We have not received the spirit of the world but the Spirit who is from God, that we may understand what God has freely given us.
> - I Corinthians 2:12 NIV

Truth is derived from the Almighty. Moreover, truth is listed as a fruit of the Spirit. Therefore, one of the effects of the fruit of the Spirit is the gift of freedom.

> And ye shall know the truth, and the truth shall make you free.
> - John 8:32

The talents are gifts to be exercised as either searching, service, or signs. In contrast the fruits are the result of a positive attitude in relationship to the Creator.

Review ━━━━━━━━━━

Address the following concepts.

1. What are the searching talents?
2. What are the service skills?
3. What are the sign abilities?
4. What are functions of signs?
5. What gifts tend to diminish with intellectual growth?

19

SPIRIT INFLUENCE

Thought
Perception is reality to you.

Check the spirits ━━━━━━━━━━

There are numerous attitudes that can sway someone's thinking. A selection of these is identified for the sake of discussion. Specific instructions are given to check out the spirit to see if they are naughty or nice.

> Beloved, believe not every spirit, but try the spirits whether they are of God: because many false prophets arc gone out into the world.
> - I John 4:1

The spirits that are discussed are predominantly from the personal branch. Another group is associated with the relations branch of angels.

A listing of some malevolent spirits shows the impressions on our mind. In some instances, the mean spirits are called demons or devils. These are negative attitudes that lead to destruction and failure.

> And the spirit of jealousy come upon him...
> - Numbers 5:14

...and whose spirit was not steadfast with God...
- Psalm 78:8

Pride goes before destruction, and an haughty spirit before a fall.
- Proverbs 16:18

Master, I have brought unto you my son, which has a dumb spirit;
- Mark 9:17

And he was casting out a devil, and it was dumb.
- Luke 11:14

...a certain damsel possessed with a spirit of divination met us, which brought her masters much gain by soothsaying:
- Acts 16:16

For you have not received the spirit of bondage again to fear;
- Romans 8:15

God has given them the spirit of slumber, eyes that they should not see, and ears that they should not hear;
- Romans 11:8

...in the latter times some shall depart from the faith, giving heed to seducing spirits, and doctrines of devils;
- I Timothy 4:1

For God has not given us the spirit of fear;
- 2 Timothy 1:7

Do you think that the scripture says in vain, the spirit that dwells in us lusts to envy?
- James 4:5

Positive attitude

The benevolent attitudes lead to peace and calm. The positive spirits lead to growth and success. Samplings of these are extracted from the Old and New Record.

But my servant Caleb, because he had another spirit with him, and has followed me fully, him will I bring into the land where into he went; and his seed shall possess it.
- Numbers 14:24

Better it is to be of an humble spirit with the lowly, than to divide the spoil with the proud.
- Proverbs 16:19

Better is the end of a thing than the beginning thereof: and the patient in spirit is better than the proud in spirit.
- Ecclesiastes 7:8

And the spirit of the LORD shall rest upon him, the spirit of wisdom and understanding, the spirit of counsel and might, the spirit of knowledge and of the fear of the LORD;
- Isaiah 11:2

Even the Spirit of truth; whom the world cannot receive, because it sees him not, neither knows him:
- John 14:17

For you have not received the spirit of bondage again to fear; but you have received the Spirit of adoption, whereby we cry, Abba, Father. The Spirit itself bears witness with our spirit, that we are the children of God:
- Romans 8:15-16

For God has not given us the spirit of fear; but of power, and of love, and of a sound mind.
- 2 Timothy 1:7

Come up here, and I will show you what must take place after this. At once I was in the Spirit, and there before me was a throne in heaven with someone sitting on it.
- Revelation 4:1-2 NIV

This overview of spirit influence on the mental pathways illustrates that each person has a choice. He can choose to let the harsh attitudes cause failure. Alternatively, he can select the good attitudes to deliver success.

Positive or negative fruit ────────────────

Fruit is the product or offspring of the parents. The offspring has the same characteristics as the parents. Therefore, it is valid to look at the fruit as both a trait and a product of the source. The fruit we display reflects who our parent is.

A very broad list of negative acts is recorded in a letter to the people in the assembly at Galatia. These deeds are a product of the negative spirits that infiltrate the mind. The negative feedback leads to destruction. The result of continuing in this atmosphere is total separation from all good.

> The acts of the sinful nature are obvious: sexual immorality, impurity and debauchery; idolatry and witchcraft; hatred, discord, jealousy, fits of rage, selfish ambition, dissensions, factions and envy; drunkenness, orgies, and the like. I warn you, as I did before, that those who live like this will not inherit the kingdom of God.
> - Galatians 5:19-21 NIV

In contrast, the positive effects come from a different mental attitude. There are no laws or limits on these caring manners. With the feedback of the control system, positive influence results in a growing physical response.

> But the fruit of the Spirit is love, joy, peace, patience, kindness, goodness, faithfulness, gentleness and self-control. Against such things there is no law.
> - Galatians 5:22-24 NIV

The fruit of the Spirit results from a positive attitude. Conversely, by developing the fruits, a positive attitude grows. These ideas were illustrated earlier as the character traits of God.

In many cases, alternate, or non-religious synonyms can be substituted for better clarification in current language. Some alternative synonyms are suggested. Theses are compassion, charisma, calm, patience, kindness, virtue, confidence, gentlemanliness, and control. Since the list is respectively in order, some terms are repeated just as filler.

To accomplish peace, power, and prosperity it is necessary to have a different mindset. In a natural condition, without the positive input, good things appear to be foolish. However, when we take on the mental philosophy of the Creator, we can judge proper decisions. This mindset it called the mind of the Anointed.

> But the natural man receives not the things of the Spirit of God: for they are foolishness unto him: neither can he know them, because they are spiritually discerned.
>
> But he that is spiritual judges all things, yet he himself is judged of no man. For who has known the mind of the Lord, that he may instruct him?
>
> But we have the mind of Christ.
> - I Corinthians 2:14-16

Weigh every thought

It is prudent to heed every thought that crosses the mind. Every idea, vision, or concept that enters your mental process may have stimulus from a spirit. So evaluate the idea to determine whether it is helpful or harmful to you. All concepts come from either the Creator or the adversary camp.

If it is a positive idea that will move you along, it is from God. When a thought is from God, he will provide a way to accomplish it in the appropriate season. If it is a negative idea that will hold you back, it is from the enemy camp. Your Father God wants to bless you as he said many times. The adversary wants to constrain you.

It's your money

Many conservative Christians misapply a statement that has become popular because of this misunderstanding.

No one can serve two masters. Either he will hate the one and love
the other, or he will be devoted to the one and despise the other.
You cannot serve both God and Money.
- Matthew 6:24 NIV

The statement is completely accurate. Unfortunately, the application
is often in error, because you can serve God and have money
without it being a master. The love of money is the problem.

For the love of money is the root of all evil:
- I Timothy 6:10

Have you noticed? People without money are more concerned and
talk about money more than the wealthy. More crime is committed
in the poverty areas than in the affluent. Therefore, the problem is
not the quantity of money one has. It is the inordinate desire for
more, regardless of the quantity.

The enemy camp is the malevolent spirit that has brought on this
warped idea about wealth. Think about the misconception logically.
If having money were bad for you, do you not think the adversary
would give you an abundance of it?

That is not the case. The malicious spirits have fallaciously
convinced many Christians that wealth is bad. Therefore, many
capable believers shun ideas of achievement, much to the detriment
to the Gospel. Success is simply making your parents and God
pleased.

As an example, look at the biblical leaders. They were wealthy or
had substantial political influence. This includes John, who lived as
a hermit, but was of the priest linage. Paul was a member of the
political power structure. Peter was an entrepreneur whose fishing
business continued while he was doing ministry work. He was able
to return to the business for an interim time. The Old Testament
patriarchs were filthy rich with large businesses and employees.

Beloved, I wish above all things that you may prosper and be in
health, even as your soul prospers.
- 3 John 1:2

Consider a very personal example. If it were not for affluence in American churches, there would not be much of the missionary outreach around the world. It is not necessary for Americans to do all the work. Nevertheless, the predominant amount of money for this endeavor is derived from within these shores. That, my friends, is one method of spreading the gospel according to God's plan.

Come again ──────────────

As we have seen, every person is being induced by external influences, both positive and negative. Each one must choose which direction he will go. The critical choice reduces to a very straightforward alternative. Accept that God came to earth in a physical form as Jesus. He lived, was slain, and came back to life three days after his burial. He returned to the ultranatural realm and sent the Spirit as a comforter and protector.

Reject this fact and the consequence is to spend forever with the adversary in the place of torment. There is a provision to escape the final judgment of earthlings that was reserved for the adversary angels. This is by pledge of allegiance to the King of kings.

> ...until the appearing of our Lord Jesus Christ, which God will bring about in his own time - God, the blessed and only Ruler, the King of kings and Lord of lords, who alone is immortal and who lives in unapproachable light...
> - I Timothy 6:14-15 NIV

A final act on the earth for the angels and mankind will be at the return of the physical appearance of God. After the return, there will be a separation between those who follow His teachings and those who reject his principles.

> When the Son of man shall come in his glory, and all the holy angels with him, then shall he sit upon the throne of his glory:
> - Matthew 25:31

For the Lord himself shall descend from heaven with a shout, with the voice of the archangel, and with the trump of God: and the dead in Christ shall rise first: Then we which are alive and remain shall be caught up together with them in the clouds, to meet the Lord in the air: and so shall we ever be with the Lord. Wherefore comfort one another with these words.
- I Thessalonians 4:16-18

This promise of a return is the positive spirit of comfort.

Our attitude reveals the influences on our loyalty. Who are all the people that can come to live in the realm of a monarch? There are only three classes. A child that is born or adopted into the family has the inheritance of the regent. A citizen that lives in the territory has certain privileges for a time, but no inheritance. An adversary rejects the authority and receives censure. Are you an heir, citizen, or adversary?

Review ──────────────

Consider these questions.

1. What is another name for angels?
2. How do spirits influence humans?
3. Who are some of the malevolent spirits?
4. Who are some of the benevolent spirits?
5. List at least 5 of the 9 fruits of a positive attitude.
6. How does a person separate between bad and good spirits?

20

WHO IS THIS GOD TO YOU?

It's your choice

A colleague once asked me a very intriguing question. When you teach, do you just give information or do you lead the group to action? That question gives the essence of the difference between a lecturer and a motivator. With that in mind, this chapter is directed to influence you to determine *Who Is This God?*

We have good spirits and malevolent spirits that are bombarding our mental processes. We must make a choice of which to follow.

As we have seen, if we follow the positive, we will excel. If we choose to allow the negative to prevail, we will pay the consequences. In the religious world, the negative action is called sin. Sin is an old English word whose perceived meaning has changed over time. It simply means choosing to reject the natural law that God originally established.

At creation, mankind was made perfect, as were all the things of the earth. Why is there not perfection now? When one-third of the spirits chose to come to earth, they brought malevolence and vice.

Their choice was to take all that was good and twist it for their own bad purposes.

When a human decides to choose the distorted rather than the best, it is called sin. Rather than sound religious, let us look at reasonable, relevant subjects. The word sin has become to be such a religious term with future ethereal implications that its impact on daily human life has been lost.

Quite simply, the concept is an offense, shortcoming, or fault. To be a fault, the action must be compared to something. To what is the fault compared? There must be principles that have overriding, universal value. There is one list of items that are unacceptable.

> These six things does the LORD hate: yea, seven are an abomination unto him: a proud look, a lying tongue, and hands that shed innocent blood, an heart that devises wicked imaginations, feet that are swift in running to mischief, a false witness that speaks lies, and he that sows discord among brethren.
> - Proverbs 6:16-19

In religious circles, there are serious or cardinal problems. There are also those that are considered mundane or ordinal shortcomings. The seven cardinal errors according to religious tradition are pride, envy, wrath, sloth, greed, gluttony, and lust. Oh what terminology to make everyone be evil. Are these faults ever specifically listed in the canon as more serious than others? No, any error is still a problem.

This concept of every person being inherently evil dates to Augustine in 412 AD. The idea is fostered basically from only one passage in the New Covenant.

> Therefore, just as sin entered the world through one man, and death through sin, and in this way, death came to all men, because all sinned.
>
> Again, the gift of God is not like the result of the one man's sin: The judgment followed one sin and brought condemnation, but the gift followed many trespasses and brought justification.
> - Romans 5:12 &16

These and the adjacent verses have been the foundation of the dogma about original sin. A historical look at this tenet shows it necessarily fostered other concepts such as infant baptism and ultimately predestination. Even a cursory look at the passage clearly states that man has problems because of his personal action, not just some inherited trait.

Planetary changes

The judgment that followed Adam's act resulted from a condemnation or curse on the earth system. This pronouncement by the Creator made changes to the way parts of the planet interacted. The basic structure stayed the same, but now there would be physical reminders of the foul impact.

> To Adam he said, because you listened to your wife and ate from the tree about which I commanded you, You must not eat of it. Cursed is the ground because of you; through painful toil you will eat of it all the days of your life.
>
> It will produce thorns and thistles for you, and you will eat the plants of the field.
>
> By the sweat of your brow, you will eat your food until you return to the ground...
> - Genesis 3:17-19

One man prompted the changes on earth because he chose to act on influence from the adversary. This permitted the malevolent or negative spirits to have an entry into the human psyche. All people who now live must contend with the thorny reminders.

Nevertheless, every person is responsible for his or her own choices. We are not inherently evil because of what Adam or our parents did. There may be some consequences for their errors, but that does not make the offspring responsible.

> Fathers shall not be put to death for their children, nor children put to death for their fathers; each is to die for his own sin.
> - Deuteronomy 24:16 NIV

The soul who sins is the one who will die. The son will not share
the guilt of the father, nor will the father share the guilt of the son.
- Ezekiel 18:20 NIV

In both Jewish and Christian tradition, a child is not responsible for
his transgressions as a youngster. If he passes to the next life in this
state, he does not suffer the ultimate penalty.

At the point he knows what is right and wrong, and makes a
conscious choice, then he is accountable. Invariably, at some point
everyone makes a wrong choice. From that time forward, he will
pay the ultimate penalty for all his errors.

Life cycle of faults ⎯⎯⎯⎯⎯⎯⎯⎯

If we are responsible for our own choices, why do we make bad
ones rather than those that help us? The theologian and legal scholar
from Tarsus, Paul, made an acerbic observation.

Now if I do what I do not want to do, it is no longer I who do it, but
it is sin living in me that does it.
- Romans 7:20

How can this be, that we do what we know we should not? How can
a God of love and compassion permit this?

A brief review of earlier observations clears it up. The Creator made
a perfect world that later had thorns and work. When originally
created, all items had a good purpose. Because of the influence of
negative, malevolent spirits, good things can be manipulated to
cause harm.

Remember that a person is born with a physical, emotional, and
mental capacity. The design of the human placed all the best options
in his structure. These are etched in the brain segment related to the
emotions.

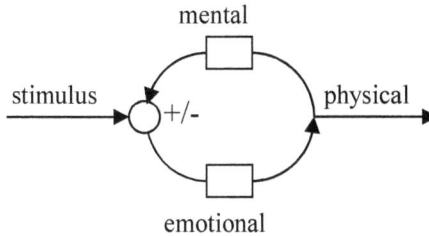

Bad influences come through the mental faculties. Because of the cyclic nature of the process, new grooves can be made on the brain paths, if thoughts and actions are repeated.

A specific example illustrates the process. Humans were created with the drive, will, or emotion for self-preservation. When a stimulus causes fright, the emotional or limbic system causes a shot of adrenalin into the body. The adrenalin provides the short-term burst of energy and reactions for physical fight or flight. This is a very desirable trait.

The negative spirit or attitude of fear can influence a person's reason. The fear becomes associated with an event or stimulus. Then, by repeated thinking about it, a disabling emotional reaction is formed that stops physical response.

For example, speaking in front of people is ranked as the number one fear, even ahead of death. Why? It is not physical harm. By repeated thoughts of what bad can happen, a person develops a fear that is not real. Fear is the opposite of faith.

Fear is what you believe will happen. Faith is what you believe will happen. Only Faith is positive.

The exercise of faith requires a season to develop. The results of faith are not immediate. Faith requires the seed to be planted, the plant to be nourished and cultivated, and the fruit to be harvested.

> To every thing there is a season, and a time to every purpose under the heaven:
> - Ecclesiastes 3:1

A season is about 91 days. This seems to transcend every activity.

The mean spirit destroys personal performance and influences you to select what is called sin. This comes by what Paul said, doing what you know you should not do.

The spirit of the opposition takes the best and influences it for bad. Nevertheless, by assenting to the Spirit of God, you can succeed and overcome.

> You are of God, dear children, and have overcome them: because greater is he that is in you, than he that is in the world.
> - I John 4:4

Courage is fear plus action. Although the spirit of fear influences people, a strong enough emotion can cause action that wins. Heroes are simply people that acted even in the presence of fear.

Meddling ─────────

Another example of malevolent influence predominates in our society. It is revealed in our dietary habits. We know that excessive quantities of certain food items are not good for us. In fact they lead to health problems and ultimately shortened life.

For example, excessive refined sugar, caffeine, salt, and saturated fat all will cause serious problems. Although it is common knowledge, most people in our society continue to over indulge. Why? It tastes good now. Human faults, in old English terminology, were called sin.

> Therefore to him that knows to do good, and does it not, to him it is sin.
> - James 4:15

It is your choice. It is not because of your environment, society, or parents. You have the consequences of your choice. By negative influence, you are constrained to less than God gave you the desire and ability to be. There was a saying during the last century that is an accurate observation - God does not make junk!

People are where they are because of choices they make.

Do something about it.

Ignorance

An old folk-saying flippantly declares that ignorance is bliss. Ignorance of principles or law is no excuse. You will still pay the consequences.

We have found in recent years that certain otherwise beneficial chemicals, medicines, and foods cause health problems. Because they had been used, people became ill from side effects. The Creator placed the reasoning ability within our mental faculties to discern problems. Therefore, even though we originally did not know they were bad, by observation we determined the challenge. We can never restore the past and its effects. We can change the present and caution about the future.

Similarly, ignorance of God's natural law is no excuse. There are consequences to rejecting its principles.

If you find something you want enough, you will change to get it. If you do not want the results enough, you will continue to be bound where you are. This is the story of the Pearl of Great Price. The monologue was revealed by God himself, teaching as the Lord Jesus, the Christ.

> Again, the kingdom of heaven is like unto a merchant man, seeking goodly pearls: Who, when he had found one pearl of great price, went and sold all that he had, and bought it.
> - Matthew 13:45-46

The process starts with a stimulus that provokes an emotion. If the dream or emotion is big enough, you will take action. You will feed the process by thinking about it. Ultimately, your action will bring the Pearl of Great Price.

The Rest of the Story ━━━━━━━━━━

A well-known commentator had a series of short radio biographies called *The Rest of the Story*. The snippets were little known biographical facts that were crowned with the name of the honoree. If we left the discussion simply with you have a choice, we would leave out the rest of the story.

Looking at the model of human behavior, we have often referred to a stimulus provoking an emotion. This caused a physical action. The mental analyzed then caused a positive or negative feedback. This caused the response to grow or diminish. The emotional and mental capacities are internal and the physical is external action. The individual is responsible for both internal and external actions.

A key ingredient that impacts the model is the stimulus or input. The person does not control this external event. If you do not cause them and have no control over them, where do they come from?

In the vernacular, stuff happens. The next few topics will look at the events.

Stimulus ━━━━━━━━━━

The most obvious stimulus or events can come from the result of physical actions by a person. The person can be someone else or it can be a previous feat by you.

Natural laws are another obvious source. For example, gravity exists in the natural law. Your emotions want something. You make a choice to heed or ignore gravity by performing a physical act.

The third source is from the supernatural realm. We do not understand many natural items, so they appear to be supernatural. In addition, people may perform outside their normal range. Those actually fit in the natural laws.

Supernatural intervention is very different. The most familiar are shields of protection from a person, physical phenomenon, or evil spirits.

> And Elisha prayed, and said, LORD, I pray you, open his eyes, that he may see. And the LORD opened the eyes of the young man; and he saw: and, behold, the mountain was full of horses and chariots of fire round about Elisha.
>
> And when they came down to him, Elisha prayed unto the LORD, and said, Smite this people, I pray you, with blindness. And he smote them with blindness according to the word of Elisha.
> - II Kings 6:17-18

Several things are obvious from this passage. First, there are events going on that we cannot comprehend. Second, if we seek to know, we can understand. Third, if we ask Yehovah as the name of Jesus, he will intervene in our affairs as we ask.

Charisma ━━━━━━━━━

The most powerful input comes simply by a gift from God. God in his infinite wisdom, power, and love knows what is good, better, and best for each person. He does actively stimulate each individual.

Paul penned perhaps one of the most eloquent passages to the Ephesus assembly.

> For by grace *(charis, 5485)* are you saved through faith; and that not of yourselves: it is the gift *(doron, 1435)* of God: Not of works, unless any man should boast.
> - Ephesians 2:8-9

Grace *(charis, 5485)* literally means joy, favor, gratitude, thanks, or pleasure. It is from the word for joy *(chara, 5479)*, which is a fruit of the spirit. Charisma *(charisma, 5486)* is an obvious extension that is always a gift. Gift *(doron, 1435)* is a present. It is significant that two different words in the passage both mean gift. It is like saying the gift is a gift.

You cannot work for the gift. To do so would be wages. The only option is to accept or reject the present. The input to you is a gift of God, now it is your choice what you are going to do with it.

The construction of the sentence in this rendition requires one point of clarification. The gift that is offered is saving. You provide faith. You do not provide work. You do not save yourself. Another translation is even clearer.

> I mean that you have been saved by grace through believing. You did not save yourselves; it was a gift from God.
> - Ephesians 2:8 New Century Version

More stimuli ─────────

If God provides one gift, he provides numerous. Every opportunity he offers is a stimulus for you to do something. Our level of achievement or accomplishment is because of constraints we have placed on opportunity.

There are numerous other practices associated with the gifts from God. Perhaps the most important practice is the concept of giving because God is the example. As you give, you will be rewarded.

> ...Let the LORD be magnified, which hath pleasure in the prosperity of his servant.
> - Psalm 35:27

> Bring you the whole tithe into the store-house, that there may be food in my house, and prove me now herewith, says Jehovah of hosts, if I will not open you the windows of heaven, and pour you out a blessing, that there shall not be room enough to receive it.

> And I will rebuke the devourer for your sakes, and he shall not destroy the fruits of your ground; neither shall your vine cast its fruit before the time in the field, says Jehovah of hosts.

> And all nations shall call you happy; for you shall be a delightsome land, says Jehovah of hosts.

- Malachi 3:10-12 ASV

Give, and it will be given to you. A good measure, pressed down, shaken together and running over, will be poured into your lap. For with the measure you use, it will be measured to you.
- Luke 6:38 NIV

In order to prosper, it is necessary to give. What are you doing with the opportunities given to you? Once given, it is your choice to receive the benefit.

We have observed a rather interesting phenomenon. Many people that follow the precepts of the Scripture are selective in its application. Some tend to separate the Old and the New as appropriate for use. This philosophy asserts that only the New is valid to present day application. Others declare that the Old promises were only appropriate for the people of Israel.

Even while applying these constraints to their belief system, they may ascribe to the Ten Commandments. The author of the most letters recorded in the New Testament also encountered this issue. He was very succinct in his charge to apply every message.

All scripture is given by inspiration of God, and is profitable for doctrine, for reproof, for correction, for instruction in righteousness:
- II Timothy 3:16

We have just examined that God gives good things to people who will accept them. Now let us look at the other options.

Why do bad things happen to good people? ─────

That is perhaps one of the most compelling questions to prick the thought of an individual. As noted above, there are inputs that come our way, other than those that are direct intervention by God. We have no control over the stimulus or inputs that come down our path. It is not our responsibility, nor is it really an option, to challenge the events that provoke us.

Nevertheless, we are responsible for what we do within ourselves. We make the choices of how we deal with circumstances. We can control our emotions and the attitudes we select in response to the events that are happening. Within the constraints, this controls the actions we take.

Someone that accepts the right spirit or attitude will have greater victory than someone accepting a bad attitude. Someone with great circumstances and abilities can blow it by taking bad choices. Conversely, someone with terrible inputs can have phenomenal victory.

It is up to you. The God of the universe gave you the greatest concept imaginable. He gave you freedom to choose whom you would serve and what you would do. What are you going to do today?

Action comes easily to some people. The critical issue is making the right action. The study gives significant opportunity to learn and know facts. It is logical that you can know more by building on what others have taught.

> Your commands make me wiser than my enemies, for they are ever with me. I have more insight than all my teachers, for I meditate on your statutes. I have more understanding than the elders, for I obey your precepts.
> - Psalm 119:98-100 NIV

What you do with the facts and how you apply them will determine your future and those you contact. A letter to a group in an ancient Greek city stimulates caution about just knowledge without expression.

> If I speak in the language of men and of angels, but have not love, I am only a resounding gong or a clanging cymbal.
>
> If I have the gift of prophecy and can fathom all mysteries and all knowledge, and if I have a faith that can move mountains, but have not love, I am nothing.

If I give all I possess to the poor and surrender my body to the flames, but have not love, I gain nothing.

Love is patient, love is kind. It does not envy, it does not boast, it is not proud.

It is not rude, it is not self-seeking, it is not easily angered, it keeps no record of wrongs.
- I Corinthians 13:1-5 NIV

The word love *(agape, 26)* can properly be rendered compassion or care. Compassion or care is an emotional concern for others with a desire to give or help them. The word is also used in the command for husbands to love your wives. It is stronger than friendship *(phileo, 5368)* without any sexual *(eros)* implications.

There is a vernacular version of the passage. "I do not care how much you know, until I know how much you care." You can have all manner of knowledge, but if you cannot relate to people, it does not matter. Your success will depend on how you relate to others.

Vulnerable ────────────

There are times that the external events are so strong that we feel vulnerable. We think we have made the right choices, but there is a gnawing feeling of insecurity. We feel overwhelmed by the circumstances and events over which we have little influence.

Dr. Bruce Wilkinson relates advice from an older mentor Dr. John Mitchell. "That feeling you are running from is called dependence. It means you are walking with the Lord Jesus."

Personally, I prefer confidence and security. However, that is not always the situation. The greatest changes and success come with that frustrating insecurity.

Thousands of years ago, a very successful individual felt this same way, but knew how to handle it. Jabez stands out in a long list of otherwise non-notable names recorded in the history. He prayed perhaps the most succinct and powerful sentence in history.

> And Jabez called on the God of Israel saying,
> Oh that You would bless me indeed, and enlarge my territory,
> that Your hand would be with me,
> and that You would keep me from evil,
> that I may not have pain,
> so God granted him what he requested.
> - II Chronicles 4:10

This thought is so crucial that it has been available throughout recorded history for you. It closely parallels the Lord's Prayer recited by Jesus to his disciples.

Think on it. Study it. Memorize it. Practice it. Depend on it. It will change your future. When things are not where you feel right, depend on the record of Jabez. It must work, since God cannot shirk from his guarantee and does not change in his relationships.

Just remember, there are no rules for you to follow to obtain the love of Yehovah. As his child and joint heir, his care is unconditional to you. It is sometimes necessary to go to your Father for advice when you do not know how to handle an event. That is great. That is dependence. That is faith. What can he do for you?

Review ───────────

Consider the following.

1. What are the three perspectives of a person?
2. What are the internal relationships?
3. What is the external perception?
4. What part of the model is outside the person?
5. Who is responsible for your choices?
6. What are the three sources of stimulus or inputs?
7. What is stimulus from God called?
8. What fruit of the Spirit is necessary for great success?

21

RECAP

Thought
*Experience is great.
I do not like getting it,
but I like having it.*
MOD

Foundations

The study of *Who Is This God?* began with the traditions of the Jewish culture. These are embodied in the book called the Bible, Scripture, or Writ. The first essays of the document were written about 3500 years ago. The latest installments were scribed almost 2000 years ago. Any document that lasts in common usage for that length of time must be taken seriously.

The Old Division was written primarily in Hebrew. The New Division was written in Greek. When any language is translated, there is the possibility of differences in shades of meanings. In addition, all languages evolve with time. The result is that English or French of today is very different from 500 years past. Again this may cause some questions on first look that are resolved with closer investigation.

The Book has lasted for millennia with general acceptance of accuracy by current users. This record makes the Book the most legitimate resource available for the topics it addresses. The issue for analysis in this treatise is God. Since God is the focal subject of the Book, the record's comments must be recognized as credible.

Triad ━━━━━━━━━━

The first area of observation is that humans are in the likeness of God. Since we cannot see God, it is logical to evaluate people for a model.

When examining mankind, we find that a person has three relationships in dealing with situations. These are emotional, physical, and mental. In old English, the terms were soul, body, and spirit respectively. A simple diagram is used to illustrate the interaction between the facets.

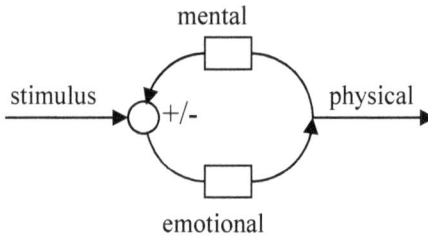

The diagram can be explained in just a few lines. A stimulus causes an emotion to move forward. The emotion promotes a physical response. The mental analyzes the response and feedback controls the emotion. The control may be positive reinforcement, which causes the physical to grow. Or it may be a negative signal, which causes the physical effect to diminish to nothing.

Similarly, God is a single entity, but he has three members. In the Hebrew record, the emotional will is called *Elohiym* and God in English. The physical person is called *Yehovah* in Hebrew and LORD in English. The mental faculty is called *Ruwach* in Hebrew and Spirit in English. In addition, a title is often used which is *Adonay* in Hebrew and Lord in English.

There is one God comprising inseparable emotional will, physical body, and intellectual spirit who interacts with people through these three relationships.

The New Tribute is initially about the physical, human life of God. The emotional element of that person is Christ or Anointed. The physical representation of the man is Jesus. The intellectual or teaching feature is Lord or Rabbi.

Another representation of the trinity is the relationship to mankind in time. Initially the emotional will was God of the Old Testament patriarchs. Then the physical person was the man Jesus of the New Testament apostles. We now have the mental characteristic of the Holy Spirit observed by the later New Testament disciples.

Still another variation of the trinity is used in the sense of a family. God is the father or procreator. Jesus is the son or physical offspring. Holy Spirit is the mental attitude that is everywhere.

Attributes

Besides the trinity, are there other ways to look at God? An attribute is a quality, trait, characteristic, or feature that describes something. Attributes of God are expressed by ideals. The three categories of ideals are philosophy, science, and personality. Each of these categories is comprised of three attributes.

Philosophy has perfect, unique, and infinite as its descriptions. Science has stable (immutable), perpetual (eternal), and everywhere (ubiquitous, omnipresent) as its values. Personality includes absolute (sovereign), self-sufficient, and all-knowing (omniscient).

Character

Two lists identify the character traits of the Spirit of God. There is one common term between the two inventories. However, the other terms are related. Therefore, the character of God is inferred from the compilation of the fruit of the Spirit.

> For the fruit of the Spirit is in all goodness, righteousness, and truth.
> - Ephesians 5:9

> But the fruit of the Spirit is love, joy, peace, patience, kindness, goodness, faithfulness, gentleness, self-control: against such there is no law.
> - Galatians 5:22-23 NIV

As discussed earlier, the understanding of some terms may vary with language and time. The current vernacular is preferred since it is more comprehensible by most readers.

The short list for character is virtue (goodness), morality (righteousness), and integrity (truth). In reality, these terms encompass all that is good and right with God and man.

The longer catalog of traits can be separated into three categories of relationships. Internal is a personal perspective. External or horizontal deals with other people. Vertical has to do with Deity.

The internal feelings are compassion (agape love), charisma (joy), and calmness (peace). The horizontal transactions are patience (long suffering), kindness, and virtue (goodness). The vertical dealings are confidence (faith), gentlemanliness (gentleness), and control (temperance). Confidence is the mental assurance that something is true.

In the name of Jesus ━━━━━━━━━━━

There is a striking parallel between the creation of earth and the birth of the God-man Jesus. The Greek version of his name is Jesus, while the Hebrew rendition is Joshua. In simplest terms, Joshua and Jesus can be stated as Jehovah *(Yehovah)* is salvation or liberator. The personal names are a direct correlation to Yehovah, the name of God.

The entire lineage of the Old Testament is the family tree leading up to this individual. The two branches of the genealogy are the royalty line and the bloodline of King David. Numerous prophesies of the Book point to this one person in history.

Many titles, tags, and terms relate to the role of Jesus as God and man. Nevertheless, his entire reason for being can be summarized into what is called the Gospel.

He was born of a virgin, he lived as a man, he taught as a prophet, and he was executed as a King. He was buried for three days, he came to life where he was seen by many, and then he ascended to heaven. There he is offering his blood as a substitute for the transgressions of any person that accepts it. As our advocate, he sits on the throne awaiting the time we will join him.

In his physical absence, he has sent a mental comforter and protector, the Holy Spirit, to minister to us.

Spirit ──────────────

The Spirit is the third and final study of God. The Spirit was at creation, is with us now, and will be involved in the future life. Spirit has access to humans through the mental pathway.

Positive spirit or attitude is from the Almighty while a negative attitude is influence by the adversary camp. From looking at the control model, we can determine that a positive mental attitude causes growth. Conversely, a negative spirit leads to destruction and demise. Filling of the spirit is a term that simply means the mental is in control over the emotional relationship.

The Spirit confers talents or gifts. These are either searching (mental), service (physical), or sign (emotional) abilities. The searching abilities are apostles, prophets, and teachers. The service talents are helpers, administrators, and most healing. The sign capabilities are miracles, tongues, and some healing.

The sign talents are part of the birthing process. Similarly, the searching capabilities are the maturing component. As the mental begins to take control, the emotional has less influence, and it may be overcome.

One substantial gift by the spirit that is not listed above in the character traits is the gift of freedom. This provides the individual with the ability to choose. The fruit of the spirit is the character traits described previously.

Law is most elegantly the identification of processes that provide security and protection. However, violating any of the natural principles will have consequences. Mankind has the option to choose to learn natural law or pay the consequences for not heeding its principles.

Spirit of another kind ━━━━━━━━━━

The Holy Spirit is the mental member of the creator God of the universe. There are numerous other spirits, commonly called angels or messengers. Spirits or angels are associated with every leadership position and with every attitude.

Humans reside in the natural realm, which is physical space. Spirits occupy the supernatural realm, which is in the same location, but is invisible. God has the ultranatural realm. Beings in a higher realm can go to a lower. However because of our reality focus, most humans are restricted from traversing or even seeing a higher realm. There are a few exceptions such as Elisha, John, and Paul. So we know humans can make the transition with the right mindset.

Angels are divided into branches based on the extent of their relationships. The personal branch operates through internal dealings with a single person. That organization has archangels over angels. The relations branch is a horizontal relationship between multiple people. That group has angels for rulers over powers. The service branch is a vertical connection with Deity. Its structure has cherubim and seraphim.

All spirits have names associated with their influence. In the canon, only three angels have human names. Michael is the archangel, Gabriel is the good news messenger, and Lucifer, was the bright star. In the Deuterocanonical book of Tobit, Raphael is the healing angel.

Angels cannot procreate with other similar beings in the supernatural realm. However, one-third chose to leave their first estate and come to earth as gods. Some of these mated with women to produce demigods and giants. The leader of the revolt had his name changed to Satan, Devil, or Adversary.

Since these chose earth as their realm of power, they are committed to the earth forever. They will ultimately be driven into the lower bowels of the earth when Yehovah returns to set up his reign.

Other gods ━━━━━━━━━━━━━━

The original source of other gods was the angels that left their first realm. Because they had supernatural powers, compared to men they appeared as gods. Virtually every culture has these super beings as part of their heritage. Genesis 6 gives the story of how the idea for these alternative deities originated.

In other cases, a malevolent relations spirit held influence over very strong men. With this authority, the men began to be worshipped. One of the originators that provided the foundation of this worship was Nimrod of Babel. Nimrod's grandmother, Ham's wife, set the groundwork for Egyptian religion. In some outside records, she is called Zeptah and she was the mother of the first Pharaoh.

The Greek titans and Olympian gods have a correlation in most other cultures. However, the Greek system of mythology has the greatest influence in western civilizations as a story of other gods.

Angel of Lord and other spirits ━━━━━━━

Angel of the Lord is a messenger that was involved specifically with a human. When God operated in the physical realm, it was as the man Jesus. Prior to that birth, his physical presence was as the angel of the Lord. These appearances are called a theophany.

The ancient scribe John gave an admonition about the various spirits.

> Beloved, believe not every spirit, but try the spirits whether they are
> of God: because many false prophets are gone out into the world.
> - I John 4:1

Numerous negative attitudes, spirits, or demons influence people. Some of these are proud, haughty, jealous, dumb, bound, fearful, lustful, and envious.

The positive attitudes, spirits, or angels also persuade the mental aspect of people. Some of these are patient, gentlemanliness, wisdom, understanding, counsel, knowledge, truth, and freedom. It is a person's choice to respond to the negative bombardment or the positive affirmation. There are consequences to going down the negative path or the positive.

Review ━━━━━━━━━

The theme of the treatise is reflected in a few queries. What is the trinity in the Old Testament? What is the trinity for the God-man? What is the trinity with time relationship to mankind? What is the trinity using family terminology? What is the trinity relationship of people? Do you maintain a positive attitude or spirit?

The review of these deliberations will tie the entire discussion together into a concise package.

Capstone ─────────

The manuscript began with a series of questions. How does the supernatural relate to people? Do you have curiosity and many questions about the supernatural? Do most books on the topics get too deep or too far out? Is there really a Creator or did the universe just happen? What are angels? Since the beginning of history, these questions have been the topics of theology and mythology.

Our objective is to take the ideas from the religious realm, then transfer the thoughts to the thinking of practical, everyday relationships.

These concepts and ideas have been tackled through a variety of examples, references, and applications. Some of the discussion required exercising your insight and evaluating your thoughts. If that occurred, the book has been a success.

Who Is This God? is about your relationship to the Creator of the universe. How is that going?

REFERENCES

Angels, Christian Information Ministries, Richardson, TX, www.fni.com/cim, 2000

George Ricker Berry, *The Interlinear Literal Translation of the Greek New Testament*, Zondervan Publishing House, Grand Rapids, MI, 1958.

Dr. Wayne Boyce, *Abstract of Systematic Theology*, Southern Baptist Theological Seminary, 1887.

L. K. Chow, *Chou Dynasty*, Honolulu, HI, 2000.

Bill Cooper, *After the Flood*, Creation Science Movement, Box 888, Portsmouth PO6 2YD, UK, 1995.

Arthur C. Custance, *The Seed of the Woman*, http://custance.org/, 2000.

Ronald E Dolan & Robert L. Worden, *China – A Country Study*, Library of Congress, http://lcweb2.loc.gov/frd/cs/cntoc.html,1987.

Lambert Dolphin, *Lambert Dolphin's Library*, http://208.55.129.251, 2000.

Dr. Marcus O. Durham, "A Universal Systems Model Incorporating Electrical, Magnetic, and Biological Relationships," *IEEE Transactions on Industry Applications*, Vol. 29, No. 2, March/April 1993, pp 436-446.

Encyclopedia Mythica, www.pantheon.org, 2000.

Dr. Billy Graham, *Angels*, Pocket Books, New York, 1977.

Dr. Henry Gray, *Gray's Anatomy of the Human Body*, 1918

Dr. Wayne Gruden, *Systematic Theology*, InterVarsity Press, Downers Grove, IL, 1994.

The Holy Bible: New International Version, Zondervan Publishing House, Grand Rapids, MI, 1973.

J. Hampton Keathley III, *Angelogy, The Doctrine of Angels*, Biblical Studies Press, www.bible.org, 1998.

241

Logos Study System, Logos Research Systems, Inc., Oak Harbor, WA, 1998.

Merriam Webster's Collegiate Dictionary, Zane Publishing, Inc., Dallas, TX, 1996.

Dr. C. I. Scofield, *Scofield Reference Bible: Authorized Version,* Oxford University Press, London, 1909.

Dr. James Strong, *Strong's Exhaustive Concordance*, Crusade Bible Publishers, Nashville, TN, 1969.

Timechart History of the World, Third Millenium Trust, Chippenham, England, 1997.

Universal Translator, software by LanguageForce.com, 2000.

William Whiston translator, *Complete Works of Josephus*, Hendrickson Publishers, 1987.

Dr. Bruce Wilkinson, *Prayer of Jabez*, Multnomah Publisher, Sisters, OR, 2001.

Dr. Spiros Zodhiates, *The Hebrew – Greek Key Study Bible: Authorized Version,* AMG Publishers, Chattanooga, TN, 1984.

AUTHORS

Dr. Marcus O. Durham brings very diverse experience to his writing and lectures. He is an engineer, who is a principal in an international forensic engineering firm. He is a Professor Emeritus at The University of Tulsa. He is a theologian, formerly Dean of Graduate Studies and Professor at Southwest Biblical Seminary.

Professional recognition includes Life Fellow of Institute of Electrical and Electronic Engineers, Life Fellow of American College of Forensic Examiners Int'l, Diplomate of Am Board of Forensic Engineering and Technology, Registered Investigator of AM Board of Registered Investigators, and recipient of Kaufmann Medal by IAS/IEEE.

His service includes international projects, missions director, teacher, professor, deacon, board of churches, and board of private schools.

Dr. Durham is acclaimed in *Who's Who of American Teachers* (multiple editions), *National Registry of Who's Who, Who's Who of the Petroleum and Chemical Industry, Who's Who in Executives and Professionals*, and *Who's Who Registry of Business Leaders*, Honorary recognition includes Phi Kappa Phi, Tau Beta Pi, and Eta Kappa Nu.

He has published over 140 papers, articles, and monographs. He has published seven books and five eBooks on such diverse topics as engineering, forensics, and theology. He has developed a broad spectrum of projects for both U.S. and international companies. He has traveled in over 22 countries and has had mentoring relationships with students in 15 additional nations.

Dr. Durham received the B.S. from Louisiana Tech University, the M.E. from The University of Tulsa, and the Ph.D. from Oklahoma State University. He had other studies with numerous institutions including Southwest Biblical Seminary.

.

AUTHORS

Rosemary Durham has equally intriguing credentials. She is a life mate who has been very involved in the family businesses. She is past President of an engineering firm and is a certified forensic investigator.

Professional recognition includes Certified Fire and Explosion Investigator, Certified Vehicle Fire Investigator, Licensed Amateur Radio, and member of Int'l Assoc of Arson Investigators. She is acclaimed in the *National Registry of Who's Who*.

Her service includes founder and president of women's mission organizations, teacher, and leader of children ministries.

She has co-authored two technical papers. She has co-authored three books on leadership, two books on theology, and two eBooks for university level classes. She has been active in traveling to over 15 countries on business and development. Her insight has been immeasurable in evaluating technical presentations and reducing them to non-technical applications.

She is a photographer, who has analyzed the photography record for over 1000 forensic projects. She has extensive training from The Crowning Touch Institute. Her credentials are Certified Advanced Color Analyst: Introduction, Intermediate, and Advanced Color analysis and Image analysis.

Mrs. Durham received the AB from Ayers Business College. She has additional studies at Imperial Valley College, Tulsa Community College, Oral Roberts University, and Southwest Biblical Seminary.

The authors can be contacted at the publisher.

⇐ ⇑ ⇒

.

www.ingramcontent.com/pod-product-compliance
Lightning Source LLC
Chambersburg PA
CBHW071955040426
42447CB00009B/1347